Truth, Tears, Turning, and Trusting

Truth, Tears, Turning, and Trusting

A Pastor's Plea to End Our Ongoing Anti-Semitism and Anti-Judaism

RON SIMKINS

Foreword by Alan Cook

RESOURCE *Publications* · Eugene, Oregon

TRUTH, TEARS, TURNING, AND TRUSTING
A Pastor's Plea to End Our Ongoing Anti-Semitism and Anti-Judaism

Resource Publications
An Imprint of Wipf and Stock Publishers
199 W. 8th Ave., Suite 3
Eugene, OR 97401

www.wipfandstock.com

PAPERBACK ISBN: 978-1-7252-6308-6
HARDCOVER ISBN: 978-1-7252-6307-9
EBOOK ISBN: 978-1-7252-6309-3

Manufactured in the U.S.A.   06/11/20

Contents

Foreword

JEWS ARE NOT A monolithic entity. I can no more speak for every Jew than I can do so for every male, or every Caucasian, or every individual who enjoys sushi. Within the congregation I serve (and even within my own family) there are a multitude of attitudes about Jewish theology and practice.

So what follows in this foreword is largely my own very personal reaction to Pastor Simkins's work in this book. It is informed by my understanding of Jewish history, tradition, culture, and theology, and I have done my best to also speak from such understandings when Pastor Simkins and I have corresponded about these topics over the past several years.

Let me start by saying that I believe in love. Here I speak not of romantic love, or even the love of a family member or dear friend (though I believe firmly in those forms of love, as well). Rather, I am thinking of what Dr. King called the "Beloved Community," or what some Christian communities refer to as *agape*: love born out of mutuality and respect. It stems from a belief that building bridges is better than building walls; that extending hands and hearts in friendship is better than retreating to our own corners and harboring suspicion and fear.

Thus, for most of the nearly seventeen years that I have served as a rabbi, I have welcomed conversation and collaboration with people from different faith traditions. I firmly believe that only by opening dialogue and striving toward understanding can we hope to confront and combat the difficult and divisive trends of bigotry and interreligious hatred that permeate and poison our society. This includes the anti-Semitism and anti-Judaism that Pastor Simkins seeks to address (and atone for) in this book.

As a Jew (again, without purporting to speak for all of my fellow Jews), I am deeply grateful that individuals such as Pastor Simkins lend their voice and their scholarship to such a heady topic, seeking to mitigate against (if not to erase or reverse) the harm done by centuries of mistrust and violence predicated upon religious differences. If readers of this book take to heart Pastor Simkins's reexamination of Christian scripture and theology; if the Jewish upbringing and practice of the historical Jesus can be better understood; if others join Pastor Simkins in atoning for hurtful acts of the past that were misguidedly perpetrated in the name of faith, then perhaps this book can serve as a catalyst for reconciliation and renewed cooperation. Perhaps it will even help readers to reclaim and recast their personal faith in a different light.

It is probably inevitable that Pastor Simkins and I do not see eye-to-eye on every argument and every conclusion that he brings forth on these pages. I am grateful that he has undertaken to write such a text, because its end goal of further cooperation and mutual respect between Christians and Jews is laudable. I am further thankful that he opened his heart and mind in conversation with me, to ascertain the perspective of one Jewish individual. Where he could do so without compromising his own closely held beliefs, he sought to incorporate my feedback and suggestions into this work. Where we continue to disagree, said disagreements should not be seen as an invalidation of other valuable insights contained in this book, nor do they diminish at all my deep respect for Pastor Simkins and his faith. It is simply inevitable that we two, who each have found a path to Truth that resonates deeply with us, must disagree about the correctness of our neighbor's Truth.

Truth, at least when it comes to faith, can be a sticky thing. In academic pursuits, truths are empirical, and two competing truths cannot simultaneously exist. For instance, I am no mathematician, but I know that in a base-10 system, $2 + 2 = 4$ and it cannot simultaneously be true that $2 + 2 = 5$. In matters of religion, however, I believe that Truth (and I purposely use a capital *T*) is in the eye of the beholder. Pastor Simkins's love for Jesus as a central figure of his faith leads him to his truth that makes him feel closer to God; I believe that my Truth, guided by Jewish tenets and lacking any theological role for Jesus, is the appropriate way for me to understand my connection to God. As unsatisfying as it may be for those of us who are conditioned to expect a *winner* in every situation, I believe that in matters of faith it is indeed feasible for multiple Truths to exist simultaneously. I am thankful to Pastor Simkins for grappling with this concept in his life, and for his setting it forth on these pages as a guiding tenet toward establishing better relationships between Jews and Christians.

The historical figure of Jesus lived and died as a Jew. Those who embraced his charismatic leadership and built a following around him, for the most part, had backgrounds in Judaism as well. New Testament authors drew from Jewish tradition and stories from the Hebrew Bible because these were the most familiar materials available to them. There is much that was Jewish about the way that Jesus lived, taught, and behaved. To this day, there remains rich opportunity for dialogue between Christians and Jews over the similarities between Jesus's ministry and Jewish practice. Pastor Simkins does well in highlighting many of those areas of overlap.

The world in which Jesus lived and died was a world of great upheaval. Many individuals were "running ideas up the flagpole," in an effort to guide the future of Judaism. Some embraced the messianic fervor attached to Jesus; others sought to move in different directions. Where I believe an unfortunate mistake was made was in the leaders of the time trying to assert a "winner-takes-all" approach, suggesting that only one Truth could prevail. For followers of Jesus, this would become Christianity; for those who did not accept Jesus's position as a fulfillment of messianic hopes, they began the path toward rabbinic Judaism. Because both felt that they had an exclusive claim to God's grace, generations of hatred, mistrust, and even violence ensued.

Jesus does not play a role in my religious practice; I don't expect that he ever will. But I still have great love and respect for Pastor Simkins and for all of my Christian friends and neighbors who cannot imagine a religious practice devoid of Jesus. Reconciliation of the type that Pastor Simkins calls for in this text does not require that any of us reject our core beliefs and values merely to appease another. Nor does it mean that we must take all of our individual theologies, put them in a blender, and content ourselves with the watered-down puree that emerges. Rather, we can arrive at a place of mutual understanding and respect that permits each of us to maintain our convictions, so long as they do not interfere with another person's free expression of their own.

The prophet Malachi asks, "Have we not all one Parent? Did not one God create us?" (Malachi 2:10). Pastor Simkins calls us to recognize that, if all people, regardless of faith, could but recognize our common place within the story of humanity, we could achieve great things and truly be worthy of God's blessing.

I pray that this work will bring us closer to such a day.

RABBI ALAN COOK
Champaign, Illinois
February 2020

Acknowledgments

MANY THANKS TO THE Jewish friends who, during the past five decades, have supported my journey, confronted me when I needed it, agreed with me and disagreed with me on many subjects, and treated me as a brother. They have taught me the importance of Truth, Tears, Turning, and Trusting in relationships between followers of Jesus and Jewish people.

Thanks to E. Paige Weston, who convinced me that I could learn to write a book if I stayed at it, and who helped me begin moving in that direction. Deep appreciation to Rabbi Alan Cook, who was kind enough to read and insightfully comment on this book, and then to graciously write the foreword. Deep gratitude also to Professor Emeritus Walter Zorn of Lincoln Christian University for reading and providing helpful comments on the book.

I am thrilled that my pastor Renée Antrosio is continuing to emphasize the themes of this book, now that our roles are reversed from when I was the pastor and she was the congregant. Rob Siedenburg has been invaluable in editing and encouraging me along the way. It has almost become cliché in acknowledgements, but it is nonetheless true that I could never have written this book without the love and support of my wife Donna, who has been with me on this journey all of our adult lives.

March 2020, Champaign-Urbana, Illinois

Introduction

It is time for those of us who claim to follow Jesus to practice what we preach. Some of us preach it most often about personal sins, such as sexual promiscuity, drunkenness, and theft. Others of us preach it most often about systemic social sins, such as racism, oppression of immigrants, and failure to provide health care. But all of us preach it in our own way—the biblical prophetic pattern of confession, lamentation, repentance, and faith. Or, as I like to say it—Truth, Tears, Turning, and Trusting. It is time. When will we walk the talk?

I am writing to plead for change—for Spirit-empowered transformation. As a pastor who has spent decades contemplating how Christians treat Jews, I urge all followers of Jesus toward Truth (confession), Tears (lamentation), Turning (repentance), and Trusting (faith that God will be with us if we move forward). It seems to take quite a lot of trusting for us Christians to tell the truth about our failures, lament them, and turn from them.

From the second century forward, and continuing today, our history has been horrendous in relating to Jewish people. We have strayed from the Jesus way. It's not just time; it's long past time for transformation. Because we cannot change the past, let's learn from it. That means now is the time for truth, tears, turning, and trusting.

There is no place for excuses when it comes to our anti-Semitism and our anti-Judaism. We have excused and exonerated ourselves for far too long. Without question, if the God presented in the Old Testament and in the New Testament is real, God wants change, and now is not soon enough!

As you read, some of you might think my approach to the Bible naïvely conservative, and others might think it not nearly conservative enough. Please do not allow those opinions to cloud the truth. We Christians—liberals, conservatives, moderates, evangelicals, progressives, charismatics, Renewal, Catholics, and Protestants—need to acknowledge our longstanding Christian Supremacy attitudes and actions. Similarly, if you think my comments are too Republican or too Democrat, do not let that become an excuse. Be assured, I do not care for either party structure very much.

This is not a plea for pretending that all religions are the same; neither is it a plea to downplay our differences. It is a plea that every person who claims a relationship with God that includes Jesus begin to act like a follower of the Jewish Jesus of Nazareth. This book is not meant to disregard our need to respond in a more Christ-like manner to people of other religions; it is meant to focus on how those of us who claim Jesus have been and are relating to Jewish people.

I believe repentance leads to joyful blessings, in this case, potential blessings beyond our imagining—blessings for us and blessings for others. I hope you will journey with me as I explore the challenges we all need to face squarely and address immediately.

1

Jesus's Jewishness—
An Inconvenient Truth?

The Need for Truth, Tears, Turning, and Trusting

No. THE INCONVENIENT TRUTH is not that Christians have expressed anti-Semitic ethnic prejudice and anti-Judaic religious prejudice for centuries. That is just a horrible truth. The apparently inconvenient truth has been, and still is, that Jesus was very Jewish, both ethnically and in his actively expressed faithfulness to the God of Abraham, Sarah, Moses, Ruth, and David.

Genesis 22:15–18 maintains that God swore to keep God's promise to bless all nations through Abraham. Based on that oath, the writer of the New Testament letter to the Hebrews believed that God's Messiah had to be Jewish, or God would be a liar (Heb 6:13–20). One might think New Testament statements such as that would cause Christians all through the centuries to celebrate Jesus's Jewishness. Reality has proven to be quite different. I am certain our church history is a reality over which "Jesus wept." I am just as sure that Jesus is still weeping over our current anti-Semitism and anti-Judaism, much of which we often do not even recognize.

What should our response be, as people who wish to follow Jesus? Truth, Tears, Turning, and Trusting. These responses were demanded by the great prophets of old, and they were a central theme in Jesus's teaching and in the New Testament writings as well. Truth about our past and present. Tears about our failures. Turning from those failures and turning toward a more Jesuslike, more humane, future. Trusting that God will bless others and us if we respond. To put this challenge in the biblical language used in many of our English translations—Confession (truth), Lamentation (tears), Repentance (turning), and Faith (trusting).

THE CONCERN IS FOR BOTH
JEWS AND CHRISTIANS.

Why is a pastor so deeply concerned about how Christians have viewed Jesus's Jewishness through the centuries and about how we continue to respond? Above all, because Jewish people have suffered horrendously due to the sins of Christians through the centuries—and this continues up to the present moment.

There are many other reasons for my concern, but one of the most salient is my conviction that God will never bless followers of Jesus as freely as God would like to, unless we lament and repent of our history toward Jewish people, as well as our ongoing anti-Semitic words and actions. I am also convinced that all forms of oppression will harm the perpetrators as well as the victims, whether we are talking about racism, misogyny, economic exploitation, or religious oppression. That is not to say the harm to perpetrators and victims is equivalent; it is to say the harm to both is real.

Yet another reason for deep concern is my conviction that this history has caused us to miss one of the most important emphases in the New Testament—the humanness of the Jewish Jesus as the fulfilment of God's purpose in creation—"male and female in the image of God" and the fulfillment of God's purpose in the covenant with Abraham's children—"all peoples on earth will be blessed through you."

By the second and third centuries AD/CE, Christian leaders were beginning to reframe their main theological question as, "How can Jesus, who is obviously God, be genuinely human?" This is quite a distance from the theological question that dominates the writings of the Jewish authors of the New Testament, which was, "How can Jesus, who is so obviously a Jewish human, be so deeply and uniquely related to God?"

Simultaneously, these early church fathers were also deemphasizing Jesus's Jewishness and increasingly presenting him as an abstract universal human. It is difficult to tell "which is the chicken and which is the egg," but I am convinced these two moves were intimately related. Both moves helped support a growing anti-Semitism and anti-Judaism in a faith community that began less than a century earlier, with a 100%-Jewish population following a Jewish human named Jesus.

FEAR AND TREMBLING COUPLED WITH LAMENT AND HOPE

Still, I write this book with fear and trembling. How can someone who is labelled *Christian* do anything other than weep in repentance over the 1,900 years of anti-Semitism (ethnic prejudice) and anti-Judaism (theological prejudice) that have been a persistent failure of the church? I could wish that some sentences were not in the New Testament, but they are. In fact, they are sometimes adjacent to sentences no one would ever wish to remove from the text. I can wish that the troublesome sentences would be heard by everyone as (I am convinced) they sounded in their original context, but that will not happen because those sentences now have a long history of being used by Christians to abuse Jewish people all around the world.

As a long-time pastor who is unashamedly a follower of Jesus, I want this book to encourage Christians to honor the faithfulness of Jewish people past and present. I also hope to address at least some of the rightful concerns of many modern Jewish people who do not necessarily identify with Rabbinic Judaism, but who do identify with their Jewish heritage and ethnicity. Still, I realize that my best effort might seem insulting to some. How can it not, given the history of Christians abusing Jews!

In his fascinating book *The Origin of the Jews*, Steven Weitzman summarizes current scholarly concerns about using the term *Jewish* to describe anyone from the first century AD/CE. It is true that the current designation *Jewish* as contrasted with the first century *Judeans* (*Ioudaioi* in the New Testament Greek) includes important changes. However, the practical reality I am addressing remains. Christian history regarding Jewish people is horrid, and that horrid attitude is reflected in the way both first century and twenty-first century *Jews* are talked about in Christian books and sermons. If Christians wish to honor the Jewish Jesus we claim to follow, we need to learn to abhor and lament our continuing failure to jettison our anti-Semitism and our anti-Judaism.

OUR PAST HAUNTS OUR PRESENT.

As I wrote an early draft of the preceding paragraphs, hundreds of white supremacists were rallying in Virginia, carrying torches and wearing swastikas. Although the organizers of the rally claimed to be celebrating the Confederacy and the Civil War and protesting the removal of a statue of Robert E. Lee, the proponents were white supremacists who target Jews, along with blacks, Hispanics, and anyone else they do not recognize as *white*. Sadly, these rallies always include white supremacists claiming to represent Christianity and *the cross*. In fact, they often pause in group prayer for the cameras, in order to be certain the identification is made. Since I wrote that earlier draft, there have been mass shootings at two synagogues on opposite sides of the United States, one of which was carried out by a church-going teenager. In fact, anti-Semitic attacks and thwarted attacks have accelerated to new highs during the 2017–2019 era. Why isn't the outcry in churches and in Christian publications much louder and much more widespread? As I continued working on this section of the book, I heard Scott Pelley of CBS's *60 Minutes* ask Starbucks billionaire Howard Schultz whether a Jew could possibly win a Presidential race in the United States. The unspoken, but clear implication? A Jewish person cannot win because far too many Christians would never vote for a Jew.

It is not just in the United States. Violence against Jewish people has again accelerated in Europe over the past few years, and once again European Christians tend to either ignore this violence—or even participate in it. A group of white supremacists in Germany now openly wear red caps with the letters *MGHA* standing for "Make Germany Hate Again." I almost retch at the horror—and I am not Jewish.

Threats to "annihilate" the Jews living in Israel are pronounced regularly in various parts of the Middle East. Tragically, even though the current threats of complete annihilation of Jews today most frequently come from individuals professing that their actions are driven by a fundamentalist Muslim ideology, Christians and Christian leaders claiming to reflect Biblical theological values have long contributed to this atmosphere of hostility toward Jewish people and toward Judaism. This unfortunate twisting of Scriptures started as early as the second century AD. Christians were a danger to Jewish people long before Muslims were.

WE CONTINUE TO READ THE NEW TESTAMENT THROUGH A LATER LENS.

Until recently, the church, including many of its best and brightest scholars, spent over 1800 years trying to erase as much of Jesus's Jewishness as possible, and in doing so, they contributed greatly to the anti-Semitism of many Christians.

Equally sadly, we have read these negative attitudes back into the New Testament writings, even though every author except Luke seems to have been a Jewish follower of Jesus. How easily those of us who claim to follow Jesus have forgotten that Jesus, and every single person who invited Gentiles to join them in the early *Jesus Movement*, was Jewish and proud of it.

We Christians soon replaced the very Jewish, human Jesus of the New Testament with haloes and European traits—and finally with American traits. We even picture those close to him—Mary, Joseph, and the twelve apostles—with their own haloes and their own Western features. What a distance from real Jewish humanness we created, when everyone around Jesus came to be depicted as not really one of us humans!

Of course, our theology followed the trend. The New Testament writings came to be thought of as *Christian* writings, rather than as *Jewish* writings about Jesus, whom these Jewish writers believed to be God's Jewish Messiah. Even the importance of Jesus's referencing Deuteronomy 6:4–5, which is the basis of the Jewish prayer *The Shema* in each of the synoptic Gospels, as well as in Jesus's high-priestly prayer in John 17, continues to be downplayed. As recently as 2015, and despite renewed scholarly emphasis on first-century Judaism as the environment surrounding Jesus and his followers, Wesley Hill (*Paul and the Trinity*) maintains that New Testament scholars give too much emphasis to the *One God* statements by Jesus, and too much emphasis to Jewish monotheism in general. Hill says this, even though the New Testament says this confession of love for "the One God" was central to Jesus's faithfulness and ours.

Art and doctrine alike continue to enhance our ability to forget that Jesus, and everyone around him, was very Jewish and very human. Jesus's Jewishness still seems to be an inconvenient truth for many.

Have you ever noticed that the Nicaean Creed around which Christian theology came to be restricted never mentions Jesus's Jewishness, his descent from Abraham, or the covenant with Abraham? Our restructuring of Christian theology around the Nicaean Creed has led most of us Christians to ignore, or at least greatly downplay, the fact that the New Testament writers present Jesus as genuinely *one of us* humans—and genuinely *a Jewish human*. In the New Testament paradigm, Jesus was human, is human now, and will always be human. This highly influential early creed provides yet one further example of how far and how quickly we moved from the New Testament emphasis on Jesus's Jewishness—apparently it was and remains an inconvenient truth.

If we were to renew our theology with the New Testament emphasis that Jesus was human, continues to be human, and will forever be human, we would be pushed toward a renewed emphasis on Jesus's Jewish heritage. The following are a few examples of the New Testament understanding that Jesus was a real human and continues to be a real human. Jesus was human: Luke 2:50–52 makes it clear that the young Jesus who journeyed with his family to worship at the Temple in Jerusalem, then continued to grow mentally and physically and to mature in his relationship with God and other humans. Jesus is human: 1 Timothy 2:3–5 describes Jesus as currently the human mediator between God and other humans. Jesus will be human—Acts 17:31 records that Paul completed his confrontation with Athenian philosophers by claiming that Jesus is the human through whom God will judge the world at the end of the age. This continuing humanity is also a theme of 1 Corinthians 15, where Paul first claims that the Messiah was raised because God always intended to raise humans from death; then Paul claims that this risen Jesus is the *second Adam/human*, through whom God is renewing his (God's) creation project of humans in the image of God—*humans of heaven*. This emphasis on Jesus's continuing humanity is a topic for another book I am currently working on, but it is important here as a reminder that Jesus's Jewishness is a fundamental part of Jesus's humanness. He is a child of Abraham, descendant of David, and Mary's son.

It is true that more recently some Jewish writers, as well as several Christian writers, have been encouraging both Jews and Christians to come face to face with just how Jewish the Jesus of the New Testament was. My personal exposure began in the 1970s with Geza Vermes's *Jesus the Jew*. I learned later that quite a few people, such as Jules Isaacs, had been preparing the way even earlier. The following statements by two Jewish scholars show that progress continues in the scholarly world toward reclaiming Jesus's Jewishness:

"Gospel Judaism was straightforwardly and completely a Jewish-messianic movement, and the Gospel story of the Jewish Christ."[1]

> Details of his (Jesus's) life, his prerogatives, his powers, and even his suffering and death before triumph are all developed out of close Midrashic reading of the Biblical materials—and fulfilled in his life and death. The exaltation and resurrection experiences of his followers are a

1. Boyarin, Jewish Gospel, 156.

product of the narrative, not a cause of it. Such creativity is most richly and compellingly read within the Jewish textual and intertextual world, the echo chamber of a Jewish soundscape of the first century.[2]

> Jesus of Nazareth dressed like a Jew, prayed like a Jew (most likely in Aramaic), instructed other Jews on how best to live according to the commandments given by God to Moses, taught like a Jew, argued like a Jew with other Jews, and died like thousands of other Jews on a Roman cross. Jesus does not have to be unique in order to say something or do something meaningful.[3]

The Christian scholar Larry Hurtado also insists on identifying both Jesus and his earliest followers as in every respect Jewish.

> The devotion given to Jesus, in earliest Christianity, is never justified or articulated with reference to the pagan polytheism of the day, with its many deities and its divinized heroes. Instead, in a novel and astonishing move that we will examine more closely later, reverence for Jesus is consistently and firmly expressed in the context of commitment to a recognizably traditional Jewish monotheism of the Roman period.[4]

Sadly, this scholarly reevaluation of Christian attitudes toward Judaism and toward Jewish people has not penetrated very deeply into the overall consciousness of many Christians. Many of our current practices and teachings are still tragically anti-Semitic and Anti-Judaism. We Christians desperately need to address what most of us are continuing to treat as an inconvenient truth.

Before directly addressing some of the practical pastoral and scholarly steps we who wish to honor Jesus's Jewishness can take, I need to acknowledge the context from which I am writing and some of the paradigms I am rejecting.

---

2. Boyarin, Jewish Gospel, 160.
3. Levine, Misunderstood Jew, 51.
4. Hurtado, How on Earth, 42.

2

My Personal Debt
to Jewish Friends and Writers

I AM NOT WRITING this book as one claiming innocence. I am a church member, and American churches have promoted white supremacy and religious supremacy—control, not trust—from the foundation of this country. I am writing as one who wishes to keep growing away from those cultural sins that have endorsed arrogance and oppression.

I want to credit my personal friends who are Jewish, as well as seven Jewish authors (out of many), for helping me see my own anti-Semitic and anti-Judaic prejudices in some of my previous understandings of the Scriptures and of church history. I have needed this help, even though I have despised anti-Semitism and anti-Judaism for many decades. The growth these friends and authors have encouraged has both deepened and broadened my understanding as I read the Bible, and this, in turn, has led me toward a deeper understanding of Jesus as a genuinely human Jewish person.

Jewish friends have greatly enhanced my understanding of—and love of—Jesus; however, I am certain both those who are followers of Jesus, and those who are not, would prefer not to be named here. On the other hand, published authors have already identified themselves publicly; so I feel free to name some of the Jewish authors who have deeply affected my life. I have decided to list them in the order in which I encountered their writings and found my thinking and my faith being transformed.

Here are the seven authors:

1. Jules Isaacs, who despite suffering the loss of his family in the Holocaust, as well as enduring many personal and professional slights during his years as a professor of history in various French universities, never quit working toward better relationships among Jews and any Christians who were open to interacting with him. When I read *Jesus and Israel* decades ago, it brought tears to my eyes over our failures as Christians in relating to caring Jewish people who have suffered unimaginable injustices at the hands of, and the silence of, *Christians*.

2. Jakob Jocz was ordained as an Anglican priest and served as professor of systematic theology at Wycliffe Seminary in Toronto. His books left me amazed that this ethnically Jewish Lithuanian embraced Jesus as his Messiah, given that he so vividly describes the anti-Semitic and anti-Judaic history of the church (*The Jewish People and Jesus Christ* and *The Jewish People and Jesus Christ after Auschwitz*). Jocz is the only person in this list who identified himself, not only as Jewish, but also as Christian—a self-identification many Christians and most Jewish people today reject, but I think Jocz must be allowed to identify himself whether one agrees with his self-identification or not.

3. Pinchas Lapide was an Israeli theologian and historian who, despite having lived through the period of the Holocaust, was determined to try to be fair in his evaluation of the validity of the New Testament's historical and theological claims concerning Jesus's resurrection. He concluded that the most coherent and consistent way to understand the historical claim that God raised Jesus from death was to acknowledge its veracity. He thought the best way to understand history was to see that God made Jesus the Messiah for the Gentiles, but

that God did not mean for Jesus to be the Jewish Messiah (*The Resurrection of Jesus: A Jewish Perspective*).

4. Abraham Joshua Heschel made it clear that the prophetic message that comes to us through the Bible "is not so much of man's concern for God as of God's concern for man." Our greatness as humans comes from the reality that God cares for us (*God in Search of Man: A Philosophy of Judaism*).

5. Amy-Jill Levine, professor of New Testament and Jewish studies at Vanderbilt, has written and edited many insightful works. Her book *The Misunderstood Jew: The Church and the Scandal of the Jewish Jesus* makes a strong case that neither liberal nor conservative Christians have yet faced how deeply some of our anti-Semitic and anti-Judaic jargon goes, nor how broadly it influences thoughts and actions all over our world.

6. Daniel Boyarin, professor of Talmudic studies at Berkeley (*The Jewish Gospel: The Story of the Jewish Christ* and *The Radical Jew: Paul and the Politics of Identity*) presents a wealth of historical background important to understanding Jesus and his times.

7. Rachel Naomi Remen (*My Grandfather's Blessings*) put me in touch with the practical day-to-day wisdom and trust of a family of Jewish believers who I think must make God very proud.

The community where I live is also blessed with a very genuine, caring, active, open-minded, and to me even more important, open-hearted, Rabbi. Although he barely knew me, he was kind enough to read an early draft of this book and respond from his personal point-of-view as a Rabbi. His comments were immensely helpful and nondefensive. Of course, there are many things in this book that he understandably disagrees with and sees very differently from the way I do; so nothing I have written should reflect negatively on him. I just want to offer kudos for his kindness that made this book better.

Along the same lines, I am not claiming that any of the authors cited above agree with what I am writing in this book, but they all wrote from a deep and highly enlightened interest in the scholarship that makes it clear that Jesus and his earliest followers were fully situated within first-century AD Judaism. What I wish to do is credit each of these authors with having drastically changed my life for the better by deepening my understanding of the relationship between God and Jesus in its Jewish context.

3

There Are No Acceptable Excuses.

PLEASE DO NOT LET ANY MISTAKES I HAVE MADE BECOME AN EXCUSE.

No DOUBT YOU WILL find as you read this book that I have made some mistakes or written some things you consider mistakes. I have never read a nonfiction book, no matter how impressive, in which I didn't find what I thought were mistakes in approach, interpretation, or application. It is easy to use these mistakes as excuses for ignoring what we do not wish to hear. I would be delighted to hear from you about any mistakes I have made. I also want to be clear that no mistake I have made provides a legitimate excuse for ignoring our continuing need for Truth, Tears, Turning, and Trusting, concerning centuries of Christian sins against *the Jews*.

PLEASE DO NOT LET MY VIEW OF SCRIPTURES BECOME AN EXCUSE.

For some, my way of relating to the Old and New Testaments might not seem conservative enough or traditional enough. For others, my view of Scriptures might seem very naïve. If, as a reader, you fall into either of these camps, please do not let that become an excuse for ignoring the plea for truth, tears, turning, and trusting. It is not an acceptable excuse.

In case it matters to you, I will attempt to be clear about the context I write from. On the one hand, I read and benefit from conservative scholars who think that somehow God controlled the writing of Scriptures far more than I think the evidence indicates. I grew up in this milieu, and I am grateful for the contributions it made to my life and faith. I believe God speaks through the Old Testament and the New Testament, when God is allowed to do so. I experience that to be true in my life and in the lives of others. I am, however, aware that the writings in our Scriptures reflect the times, cultures, personalities, and limitations of the authors, as well as the hand of God. I find the wooden views of inspiration that attempt to eliminate the human dimension from Scriptures not only to be obviously wrong-headed, but also to rob us of the wondrous reality that God is willing to relate to real humans with real cultural and personal limitations. Far from scary, that reality gives me confidence that God is willing to be involved with people like me—and like you.

On the other hand, I read and honor the insights of the more skeptical strand of scholarship and have benefited greatly from some of the important understandings they have produced. Still, I am far less skeptical than many current scholars, pastors, priests, and rabbis are concerning the claims in the Old Testament and the New Testament that describe interventions by God in human history, as well as acts of faithfulness on the part of various humans. I am not convinced by the paradigm that reconstructs Biblical narratives as though they were mostly the creations of, rather than the relatively accurate historical memories of, later generations.

Of course, absolute proof of any historical claim rarely, if ever, exists. However, I do find the modern reconstructions that deny that most of these Biblical claims are historically based to be reconstructions flowing from philosophies that begin with assumptions of nonvalidity, rather than claims based in evidence that necessarily compels. In short, I trust those who wrote and edited the Scriptures far more than I trust many of those of us who reconstruct them today. Why? Partly for an experiential reason. God uses them so powerfully to transform my life and the lives of others, when we allow God to do so. But there is also what seems to me to be an important logical reason. I think C. S. Lewis's experience, recorded in one of his lesser-known works, *Christian Reflections*, should be taken seriously.[1]

As a prolific British author, Lewis maintained that critics who shared his culture, his time in history, and his language rarely, if ever, managed to reconstruct correctly his motives and his processes as an author. Given that reality, he thought it even less likely that reconstructions claiming to accurately assess the motives and processes of authors whose writings come from a different culture and a different time, and which were written in a different language, should be regarded as overwhelmingly accurate reconstructions. He concluded that these reconstructions seem more accurate than our current attempts at reconstructing the motives and processes of contemporary authors only because the ancient authors are long dead and cannot provide any correctives.

My reason for bringing my approach to Scriptures into focus at this point is not to argue an issue that already fills the pages of many books. I bring it up in an attempt to be transparent, and then to appeal to you as my reader to not discount the many pleas in these pages for Christians to lament and repent, just because you might think my approach to the New Testament is too liberal or too conservative—too progressive or too evangelical. What you think of my understanding of the Bible provides no legitimate excuse for ignoring our need for Truth, Tears, Turning, and Trusting concerning centuries of Christian sin against *the Jews*.

PLEASE DO NOT LET MY EMPHASIS ON THE JEWISH CONTEXT OF THE NEW TESTAMENT BECOME AN EXCUSE.

Although I am going to argue later that the writers of the New Testament were neither anti-Semitic (demeaning Jewish ethnicity)

---

1. Lewis, Reflections, 159–161.

nor anti-Judaism (demeaning Jewish faithfulness), prior to doing so I need to acknowledge some important realities. First, for various reasons, many Christians and many Jewish people might find my emphasis on Jesus's Jewishness and on the Jewishness of the New Testament frustrating. For Christians. it can seem to diminish Christian superiority. For Jews, it can seem to erase an important and necessary line between Jewishness and Christianity.

Second, in several practical ways, the Jewishness of the New Testament might not matter very much to a Jewish person today. Jews today live in the world that Christian readers of those early texts have helped to create by reinterpreting the early texts. None of us live in the world the New Testament authors wrote in. We live *now*; we do not live *then*. And the *now* readings of the New Testament texts are often fraught with anti-Semitism and anti-Judaism.

Nothing I write later about the first-century context is an attempt to excuse church history. Neither is anything I write an attempt to excuse the hurtful mistakes I personally have made and undoubtedly will yet make in relating to Jewish people. And, although it is my goal to become completely free of anti-Semitism and anti-Judaism, only Jewish people can tell me how well I am succeeding in my quest. I was born and bred in an environment fed by centuries of White European Supremacy and Christian Supremacy. I hope that the resulting blind spots are in the process of being healed and eliminated. How far I have progressed is best judged by listening carefully and nondefensively to input from Jewish people.

Having said that, I do think it can be helpful in Jewish–Christian relationships to see that the texts would not have sounded either anti-Semitic or anti-Judaic in their original historical settings. However, this does not excuse Christians today from confessing, lamenting, and repenting of our past and present sins. Neither does it excuse us from learning how we can better handle these texts that we cannot avoid. They are there, and they are our texts. Unquestionably, they sound terrible in the modern world that the church helped to create. No matter how they sounded in the first century, we must deal with how they sound now in the light of the sins of Christians and the Church. There is no excuse for attempting to excuse the inexcusable.

PLEASE DO NOT LET THE FOCUS ON JEWISH-CHRISTIAN RELATIONSHIPS BECOME AN EXCUSE.

I expect some readers will already be feeling frustrated by my singling out the need for those of us who claim to follow Jesus to repent from our attitudes toward Jews and Judaism. If you are feeling that my focus is far too narrow, I find that reaction to be quite understandable. After all, to vastly understate reality, we Christians have not had a great track record in relating to people from Muslim backgrounds, Native American religious backgrounds, African religious backgrounds, Hindu backgrounds, etc. I do find each of these failures tragic, and each entails a need for truth, tears, turning, and trusting on the part of Christians for the ways we have dehumanized those we have labeled as *other*.

In fact, I am rather certain that if Jesus were invited to speak in many American churches today, he would retell his story about the compassionate ("good") Samaritan, recorded in Luke 10, in terms of a compassionate Muslim saving a Christian from a situation in which a Christian theologian, a Christian Bible scholar, a Christian pastor, and a Christian priest looked the other way. In other churches, he would have an illegal border-crossing Liberation-Catholic Mexican of Native American origins save a white evangelical fundamentalist Arizonian Protestant, whom Sheriff Arpaio did not find time to help because he was busy chasing immigrants in order to "save America."

Having said that, the rest of the issues between Christians and other religions, even Muslims, with whom both Christians and Jews share some roots, as important as they are, are different from the issues between followers of Jesus and Jewish people. Jesus was a faithful—*observant* in many ways—Jewish believer and worshipper. The New Testament still identifies him as "Jesus of Nazareth" and as "the Son of (Jewish King) David." Right or wrong, the early Jewish followers of Jesus invited non-Jewish people into a new understanding of "Israel" and demanded an acceptance of the Jewish Old Testament as the context for understanding the relationship between God and Jesus. It is Jesus's Jewishness that makes it uniquely important to unpack how the Christian tendency to deemphasize his Jewishness has also caused us to deemphasize his genuine humanity, and, in doing so, to demean his very human relationship with the One God, which is so central to his heritage and to the Hebrew Bible. As is so often true, in demeaning and oppressing others, we manage to wound ourselves as well.

4

Christian Fundamentalist Zionism

Is Neither Confession Nor Repentance.

THE NATION OF ISRAEL AND CHRISTIAN ZIONISM

I THINK I UNDERSTAND, at the level a non-Jewish person can, how important the existence of the nation of Israel is to many Jewish people. After about 18 centuries of being treated badly by most Christians and by most Europeans, 14 centuries of being treated badly by many Muslims, and another century of being treated badly by Nazism and by most communist nations, Jewish people find little reason to entrust themselves to the international community. The existence of Israel provides at least a bit of survival security for many Jewish people in a world where anti-Semitism and anti-Judaism have run rampant for centuries. Those of us who are not Jewish seem to easily forget, and Jewish people rarely forget, that pre-Nazi Germany was probably the most advanced nation in the world in terms of science, philosophy, military, Christian academic studies, and the integration of Jewish people into most levels of society.

In a world with such an anti-Semitic history, any criticism of the modern state of Israel can easily be heard as a criticism of Jews and Judaism, and it is, in fact, often used exactly that way around the world. So, I write the next few lines with a sense of being on a precarious ledge. Still, though thanking God for the existence of the state of Israel, I also find it necessary to disassociate what I am writing from the approach many fundamentalist Christians in the United States take in regularly rubber stamping any action taken by the state of Israel as justified and as a fulfillment of Biblical prophecy. Like many of my Jewish friends and like many Jewish authors, I am quite aware of the injustices sometimes perpetrated by the modern nation of Israel toward Palestinians, just as I am aware of the unwarranted attacks by some Palestinians on Israelis. Israel certainly enacts no more injustices in the name of "national security" than does my beloved United States, but not as few as one would wish, either.

Christian Zionism in the United States tends to be almost mindlessly pro-Israeli, as it attempts to defend anything modern Israel does. This is justified by these Christians through their belief that the Old Testament and the New Testament promise a restoration of the state of Israel as a precursor to Jesus's return, and "rapturing" these Christians away from an upcoming time of "terrible tribulation" that is about to come upon the world. In the minds of these Christian Zionists, the sooner Israel becomes first devastated and then victorious, the more quickly they can themselves, as Christians, escape future bad times. Thankfully, most Israelis appreciate the political support but know not to trust that it will be there the moment these fundamentalist Christians no longer see Israel as a support for their strange self-centered doctrines.

"LEFT BEHIND" THEOLOGY

Christian Zionism based on "rapture" theology is broader than the "don't be left-behind" movement of recent decades; however, the popularity of the "don't be left behind" movement is its most recent and most dangerous incarnation. This book cannot address at length the foolishness of the "don't be left behind" theology, but I will make four important points.

1. It is ironic that a people who claim to follow a God who allowed his Messiah-Son Jesus to be brutally and unjustly executed on a Roman cross think that God's main goal in current history is to spare them from intensely difficult times!

2. It is not surprising that this kind of theology tends to arise primarily among privileged groups who have enjoyed relatively easy lives, compared to the rest of the world. If you asked followers of Jesus in Egypt today, in China today, in Uganda under Idi Amin, in Russian Siberia under Stalin, or those living anywhere in the Middle East where Da'esh has been successful enough to stage crucifixions and beheadings of Christians, you would find followers of Jesus who know that the "great tribulation" is always occurring in their part of the world. Certainly, Da'esh (often identified as ISIS, although it does not represent most Muslims) has slaughtered many more Muslims than Christians, but my critique here concerns "*rapture theology.*" The sufferings of Christians (and non-Christians) in the world might or might not get worse, but we certainly need not wait for the future to see "great tribulation" caused by the "*beastliness*" of world empires, often supported by the "*beastliness*" of powerful religious systems and structures (see Revelation 13 and Daniel for this imagery of political and religious beastliness).

3. The "rapture" and "left behind" theology of many modern Christians is a recent phenomenon historically, and it is supported through misusing a few New Testament texts with no regard for their overall context. Apparently it began with a charismatic vision experienced by a young woman in a nineteenth-century prayer meeting in Scotland, and it was then picked up and championed in the footnotes of English Bibles published by Darby and Scofield. From that point forward, it began to be read into the Biblical texts by many Christians, until the initially strange interpretation became unquestioned doctrine for many. This "rapture" theology was then exported around the world by English-speaking missionaries.

   The "rapture" is supported through misusing a few New Testament texts with no regard for their overall context. There are several of these misused texts, but the two most influential have been 1 Thessalonians 4:13–18 and Matthew 24:40–41.

The Thessalonians passage pictures Jesus's return to rule on earth as one in which he and his entourage will be greeted by his living followers, who will then escort him into his reign on earth. This description is a cosmic reenactment of scenes such as Jesus's "Triumphal Entry" into Jerusalem and Solomon's triumphal entry into his reign in Jerusalem. First-century readers would have been familiar with this same scene when the locals went out to meet the Caesars and their entourages and escorted them into the city as the beginning of great celebrations. The residents of my home city did something similar when our dignitaries caravanned out to meet former President Obama and his entourage and then escorted him from the airport to campus as graduation speaker.

I remember a similar picture at a personal level when dozens of family and friends gathered at the airport to meet my parents when they returned from almost a decade as missionaries in two African countries. We wanted to be there to meet them as they arrived, not to go with them back to Africa, but in order to then escort them to our homes.

"Rapture" away from earth was never in the picture for writers who trusted Jesus would be sent by God to reign on God's earth and to transform the kingdoms of the world into the kingdom of God. The goal is not to escape earth, but to see it re-created as the place where God can dwell face to face with humans, as God's renewed forever human family. Not only was this the prophetic anticipation of God's future reign on earth announced in the Old Testament by several prophets, it was reiterated in New Testament writings such as Revelation 5:10, 11:15, 21:2–3, Matthew 5:5, and Romans 8:20–24. The goal is not escape to heaven; it is heaven coming to earth!

The other most-often misused Scripture is the source of the phrase "Don't be Left Behind." Somewhat ironically, Jesus's words actually imply that you *would* wish to be among those who "are left." When Jesus spoke of those who would be "left" as God brought judgment (Matt 24:40–41), he drew the word "left" and the imagery from the flood account in Genesis 7:23. Those "left" were those spared from the judgment expressed in the flood event. Surely Jesus was using the word the same way as the text he referenced and those "left" behind are those who are *not* "taken" by judgment. This way of understanding the passage fits Jesus's immersion in the writings of the Old Testament prophets and poets who promised that the future of the earth belongs to "the humble who will inherit the earth" and be "left" to enjoy God's gift of "new heavens and new earth" forever (examples include Ps 37:9, 11, 22, Prov 10:30, and Isa 65:17–25). This also fits Jesus's teaching that the meek will someday inherit the earth (Matt 5:5). Rapture theology and its "left behind" theme flow from one misunderstanding piled upon another.

4. Ironically, the rest of the theology of most "don't be left behind" Christians is in its fundamental beliefs decidedly anti-Synagogue and anti-Judaism, while often giving voice to anti-Semitism as well. Most of these Christian fundamentalists do not think that God will honor the faithfulness of even one Jewish person, no matter how deeply godly and urgent in seeking God, if that person does not agree with the Christian fundamentalist that Jesus is God's Messiah before he or she dies. In fact, Christian Zionism tends to see the Jews as pawns through whom God will prove Christian superiority. Those Christian Zionists who also believe in "the rapture" present Jews as tools to bring about Jesus's return, at which time "the Jews" will be apocalyptically eliminated as a unique people. Contrast this with Paul's perspective in Romans 11:26 that sees Jewish people as an identifiable people throughout human history: And so all Israel will be saved, as it is written: "The deliverer will come from Zion; he will turn godlessness away from Jacob."

I am not suggesting that eradicating the substantial influence of the Christian Zionism of the "Left Behind Movement" would suddenly make it clear how a follower of Jesus should view the many issues of justice and security that daily haunt the lives of

Palestinians and Israelis. The results of centuries of European Co-lonialism have created what appears to be an almost insoluble mess in the Middle East.

Neither am I suggesting that the so-called "Biblical borders" issue in which Christian Zionists advocate for modern Israel to have the same territory as God gave the Israelites according to Old Testament would suddenly become clear without "left behind" the-ology. It isn't clear for me personally. But I am glad to leave that resolution in the hands of God, rather than in the hands of the vari-ous military forces of the world. Meanwhile, because many Ameri-can Jews favor some form of the "two-state solution," it is certainly not anti-Semitic or anti-Judaism to think that solution might lead to as much justice as we seem capable of in the current realities of our modern world.

The one thing I am confident of is that "the Jesus Way" will bend toward supporting as much grace, mercy, and justice as pos-sible, not toward increasing violence. Jesus rejected again and again using, and misusing, Old Testament texts as an excuse for hating the enemy and attempting to violently destroy them. I am confident that, in the same way, the living Jesus today rejects the way Chris-tians use New Testament texts as an excuse for arrogance, hatred, and violence.

5

Some of What We Need to Confess and Lament

THE ANTI-SEMITISM OF OTHERS NEVER EXCUSES US CHRISTIANS.

HATRED OF THE JEWS by some people predates both Jesus and the later development of *Christianity* by centuries. Much about Jewish *otherness* in relating to God, one another, and people of other backgrounds seems to have rankled some ancients at times—especially when it touched their egos or seemed to threaten their systems of dominance. The perceived Jewish threat to systems of dominance runs throughout the Book of Daniel. The personal hatred this threat to dominance could generate by insulting the ego is portrayed in the book of Esther and is evident in the orations of the famous and influential Roman, Cicero. Anti-Semitism has sometimes been identified as "the world's oldest hatred." Maybe. Maybe not. What should be clear is that it is never permissible for followers of Jesus to excuse our own sinfulness by pointing at others as "just as bad" as or "worse" than we are.

If scholars such as James Carroll (*Constantine's Sword: The Church and the Jews, A History*) are correct, the population of Jewish people during the Roman Empire would predict a current Jewish population on the earth today of more than 200,000,000 Jewish people rather than the actual worldwide Jewish population of around 14,000,000.[2] Christians, Muslims, Atheists, Nazis, and Communists can all take their share of the blame for this tragedy, but anti-Semitism by Christians ranks right up there with the worst of culprits.

Although I differ greatly from James Carroll's way of understanding the claims of the New Testament concerning Jesus and Judaism, one can only weep and plead for undeserved mercy and forgiveness as one reads his description of the development and enactment of anti-Judaism and anti-Semitism through the centuries of *Christian* political dominance in the Western world, beginning with Emperor Constantine. Reading the works of Jakob Jocz (see chapter 2), who has a much higher view of the New Testament and of Jesus than does Carroll, leaves you praying the same desperate lament, wondering if God can possibly find enough mercy and forgiveness for the way the Church has treated Jewish people.

CHURCH ANTI-SEMITISM—ONE OF OUR ORIGINAL SINS

How different might history have been if the early church fathers had acknowledged in their interpretation of the scriptures and their understanding of their identity as followers of Jesus the ongoing indebtedness every follower of Jesus has to our Jewish roots! In fact, following Jesus makes no sense at all except as an extension of the privileged status of Jews as the bearers of God's special self-revelation to those who are not ethnically Jewish.

To be clear: I am not overstating the anti-Semitic and anti-Judaic theology and attitudes of the so-called *church fathers.* If anything, I am understating it.

2. Carroll, Constantine's Sword, 26.

It is very easy to document the anti-Judaism and the growing anti-Semitism of the early church, beginning as early as the second century AD, and continuing through the centuries. It is also easy to document the early transition from emphasizing Jesus as God's fulfillment of God's purpose for humanity toward emphasizing Jesus, not as a Jewish human, but primarily as *God* and as an abstract universal human. As mentioned earlier, I do not think the development of these two parallel reconstructions of the New Testament teachings and their grounding in the Old Testament is an accidental parallel. The more Christians overemphasized "Jesus is God," the more they felt free to deemphasize "The human Jesus is Jewish."

Tragically, it is also far too easy to document the continuing anti-Semitism and anti-Judaism that is pervasive throughout the church world today. Many have done extensive and scholarly documentation of this reality. A few examples with varied approaches include Amy-Jill Levine's *The Misunderstood Jew*, Jakob Jocz's *The Jewish People and Jesus Christ: The Relationship between Church and Synagogue*, Jules Isaacs's *Jesus and Israel*, and James Carroll's *Constantine's Sword: The Church and the Jews, A History*.

Through the centuries, as Christians gained political and military power in the West, the tragic costs of anti-Semitism grew. It is a dishonest confession, if the goal is to let the rest of us off the hook, for Christians to say things like, "But those anti-Semites were not 'real' Christians." Perhaps some were not "real Christians," and perhaps many were very misguided Christians. Nevertheless, we Christians in the Western world have for centuries been socially and legally privileged over most Jewish people because of this horrible history. We all need to repent publicly and lament our sinfulness as the church, not attempt to distance ourselves.

I am not sure that Rodney Stark (who has written several insightful books) is correct in arguing that Christians were no worse, perhaps even better, than many others, but I am positive that his attempt in *For the Glory of God* to justify the crusades, the witch hunts, and the inquisition as not so bad as others is wrongheaded if it leads to our excusing ourselves. Being no worse than others in our hatreds, prejudices, and violence is certainly not an expression of Jesus's way! It isn't even a worthy expression of basic human morality.

True, the Old Testament book of Esther tells us that virulent anti-Semitism and anti-Judaism preceded the church fathers. It appeared again under the Seleucid ruler Antiochus Epiphanes (see 1 Maccabees), and we also see it demonstrated in various ways in Greco-Roman literature prior to the time of Jesus. Even though (perhaps partly because) Jewish expressions of faith and custom had been granted some unusual leniency under Alexander the Great and under Roman law, there was also a lot of bitterness in the Greco-Roman world toward the Jewish people—a fact that the Roman orator Cicero makes quite clear. Having said that, the fact that the church fathers did not invent anti-Semitism does not excuse the fact that theologians and churchmen, who claimed the Jewish Jesus as their Lord, incorporated anti-Semitism and anti-Judaism into their pastoral and theological instruction. Many of our early church leaders spoke slanderously of Jesus's people while attempting to disassociate Jesus from his Jewish people and his Jewish humanity.

"OUR" FATHER . . . FORGIVE US "OUR" SINS. . . .

We need to be lamenting our sins, not attempting to excuse ourselves as Christians. We need to be repenting, not looking for ways to justify Christianity. Those of us who want to disassociate ourselves from the tragic failures of the church—"they were not real Christians as we are"—without first lamenting openly, clearly, and publicly "our sins," are not doing God or Jesus any favors. We are corporately a part of these sins, and we also have often been the benefactors of the dishonest gains and social prerogatives that flowed from them.

Daniel understood this corporate sinfulness and the need for including ourselves in the repentance. As a Jew, he laments the sins of Israel in Daniel 9 as "our sins" even though he personally abhorred them. Ezra's prayer as recorded in Ezra 9 makes clear that Ezra identified with and repented for Israel's shame and failures even though he abhorred them. I think Jesus was enacting this same understanding of corporate guilt and the need to repent as a member of the institution/nation/church when he responded to John's call for Israel to engage in a baptism of repentance. He ignored John's attempt to encourage him not to join in maintaining that he needed to do so to be "righteous" or "right with God" (Matt 3:15).

Isn't this responsibility to confess and lament our corporate sins one of Jesus's central teachings about our prayer life and relationship with God? Do we hear ourselves, as all over the world we repeat: "*Our* Father . . . forgive us *our* sins. . . ."?

That I personally disagree with what the church did, and that I fervently hope that I might be one of the followers of Jesus who would have reacted differently in the past does not change the fact that I am still a part of the community that has a history. I am still a part of a community that attempted to leverage its privileged status at the expense of "the Jews." I cannot be free of its sins without first acknowledging them as "our" terrible failures—Daniel could not, Ezra could not, Jesus could not, and we cannot.

CHURCH LEADERS, ANCIENT AND MODERN, CONTINUE PROMOTING PREJUDICE.

Past and present, our best and brightest Christian scholars have intentionally and unintentionally promoted Anti-Judaism and Anti-Semitism.

It is true that the Jewish revolt against Rome that brought about the destruction of the Temple in 70 CE likely alienated some Jewish people and some Jewish followers of Jesus from one another. It does seem to be true that at least the leadership of the emerging church and the leadership of emerging Rabbinic Judaism were beginning to think of themselves as two separate communities by the end of the first century AD. (See James D. G. Dunn's *Jews and Christians: The Parting of the Ways: AD 70–135*.) This differed from the earlier tension, which was between two communities vying for influence within the same Jewish milieu.

Within 100 years, the church moved from Paul's understanding—that what God had done in Jesus opened the possibility for Gentiles to be included in "Israel" (the covenant with Abraham)—to the church fathers' understanding—that the same Biblical texts were proof for the claim that God had now broken the covenant with Jewish people and excluded Jews from "the true Israel," an act Paul had maintained God would never do (Rom 11:1 and 11:26).

Soon, it was not only early heretics like Marcion who wanted to remove all Jewishness from the New Testament, but reputable church fathers like Chrysostom and Augustine, who were virulently anti-Semitic and anti-Judaism. Around the beginning of the fifth century, Chrysostom preached eight sermons that, among other even more horrendously anti-Semitic statements, not only damn "the Jews," but damn any Christian who would celebrate the Passover Seder with Jewish people.

The fact that Chrysostom's sermons damn me for the many Seders I have celebrated with my Jewish friends does not concern me nearly as much as the sins of Christians against Jews his sermons have encouraged. They have stoked the fires of anti-Semitism in many churches through many centuries. Importantly, Chrysostom wrote those sermons because at least some Christians and Jews were, to Chrysostom's chagrin, still getting along with one another quite well. In fact, though the leaders of the two groups had long ago parted ways, Rodney Stark mentions archaeological findings that indicate that Jews and Christians shared worship buildings and apartment buildings well into the fifth century AD in some parts of the world (*The Rise of Christianity*). This camaraderie, among worshippers of the same One God, seems to have intensely bothered some early Christian leaders.

Unfortunately, Chrysostom was far from unique among church leaders. A bit later, Augustine describes the Jews as those with the "mark of Cain," who continued to exist as unwilling witnesses to God's judgment on their rejection of Jesus. (This was also a misunderstanding of what Genesis said was the purpose of the mark of Cain—an answer to Cain's prayer for mercy and protection from the violence of others.) Augustine's approach that was meant to stop Christians from killing Jews by labeling Jews as a permanent witness to God's rejection of Judaism and choosing of Christianity is a sad example of the old adage, "With friends like this, who needs enemies?"

We could add the earlier Tertullian, who in his day was deeply influential in the theology of the church, even though later he was condemned as too radical. Unfortunately, this "too radical" judgment of Tertullian by the church did not extend to his views concerning Jews (or women), and he, too, encouraged the sad trajectory of the church toward increasingly anti-Semitic attitudes and interpretations of the New Testament writings.

Anti-Semitism and anti-Judaism continue throughout church history (see Jakob Jocz's heartbreaking book *The Jewish People and Jesus Christ: The Relationship Between Church and Synagogue*) right up into modern times. Two recent popes—John XXIII and Francis—though hardly going as far as we need to go, are at least heart-warming exceptions to the more common tendency of papal authority to either justify anti-Semitism or repent in a manner that is designed primarily to exonerate and excuse Catholic Christians and the Catholic Church.

Lutherans, and many other Protestants, mostly ignore Luther's sinful anti-Semitic tirades, rarely publicly repent for them, and tend to greatly understate his impact on the spiritual climate that led to Nazism.[3] Only a generation ago, Christian scholars who had seemed to be good friends turned their backs on Jewish peers as the Nazi spirit swept Europe. For me, it is heart-rending to read the work of the Jewish scholar Jules Isaacs (*Jesus and Israel*), in which he describes his deep respect for the Jewish Jesus and his tragic surprise as his fellow scholars abandoned him to his fate when he was attacked by virulent anti-Semites. He naively thought the Christian professors with whom he collaborated in his French university were genuine friends, whose integrity would never allow him to be blackballed just because he was Jewish.

As Amy-Jill Levine notes, converts to conservative Protestant missions around the world tend to learn anti-Semitism from the missionaries. As she further notes, liberal Protestant scholars also tend to teach anti-Semitism, without intending to do so, by setting up observant Judaism as the foil for their liberal reconstructions of Jesus as their champion for ignoring religious guidelines and

---

3. Luther, The Jews.

structures (*The Misunderstood Jew*). Their anti-Judaism tends to also unintentionally promote anti-Semitism.

Furthermore, and without denigrating the helpful contributions that historical criticism of the Bible has made in many areas, it is important to remember that many of its current theories and assumptions originated in a German, British, French, and then American climate of rampant anti-Semitism. These scholars often did not want Christianity to be about a Jewish "Messiah," but rather about a Gentile "Christ." At minimum, the assumptions underlying much of the scholarship of that era need to be reevaluated due to their implicit, and often explicit, anti-Semitism.

N. T. Wright summarizes some of the implicit anti-Semitic assumptions of European Enlightenment scholarship:

> Following Hegel and other Enlightenment thinkers, and combining that train of thought with a Lutheran reading of Paul in which "Judaism" represented the wrong way of doing religion, "Jewish" ideas were regarded as at best inadequate and at worst dangerous. The history-of-religion school a hundred years ago was eager, in its rejection of all things Jewish, to "derive" Paul's view of Jesus from the pagan environment in which there were many *kyrioi*, "lords": Jesus was simply a new one, a cult deity with certain specific features. Paul (on this view) purposely abandoned the Jewish category of "Messiahship."[4]

As Wright also notes, a lot of current Biblical and historical scholarship is focused on just how Jewish Jesus was and is attempting to locate him in his time and place as a Jewish person of the Jewish Second Temple and Roman Imperial era. But even in the scholarly circles attempting to take Jesus's Jewishness and that of his early followers seriously, there has not been an accompanying attempt to reevaluate the impact of anti-Judaism on many assumptions implicit in modern Biblical criticism.

In my opinion, even the late dating for the New Testament writings that originated mostly with German and British scholars, many of whom were quite openly anti-Semitic, should be

4. Wright, *Paul and Faithfulness*, 645.

re-evaluated. We see in all fields of study that the basic assumptions researchers begin with deeply impact the *logical* results of research. It was easy for anti-Semitic scholars to contemplate a New Testament that was written in the late first century or early second century, by writers who were severed from the early Jewish roots and who present us with a non-Jewish (even anti-Jewish) Jesus. Often we humans, including our scholars and scientists, find the results we wish to find in our research. Unfortunately, even today, many New Testament scholars, who do not wish to be anti-Semitic, still do not go back and question the effect of anti-Semitism and anti-Judaism on the assumptions that underlie the late dating of the New Testament materials. A fresh approach might lead to major revisions in the *accepted* scholarship concerning what we *think we already know.*

In *Paul and the Faithfulness of God,* N. T. Wright has also given a very insightful summary of Paul's overview of Israel's history and his belief that it had been fulfilled in a special and overwhelming manner in the life, death, and resurrection of Jesus the Messiah of Israel. He shows that Paul did not, and never would have, entertained the thought that God had "replaced" Israel with something new called "the church." He also shows that when Paul bitterly critiques those Jewish leaders whom he believed were intentionally attempting to mislead their people concerning what God has done in Jesus, Paul was critiquing his own former thoughts and actions as a zealous opponent of the Jesus Movement.

I wish that Wright had also been clear that Christians should honor the amazing faithfulness toward God of many Jews then and today. Sadly, this scholar and historian, to whom I personally owe a great debt for many insights, does not seem to have fully faced up to our continuing failure as followers of Jesus in our relationship with Jews. He briefly acknowledges the "rotten track record" of "churches of all sorts" regarding Jews "in the last half millennium, at least." He then seems to excuse not paying more attention to God's faithfulness toward the Jews during the past two millennia, or to the faithfulness of many Jews toward God during that same history, by saying "history is basically what this book is about."[5] However, "history" did not end in the first century, and the "history" of the past 18 centuries records the ongoing "faithfulness of God" in the lives of many Jewish people, and the ongoing faithfulness of many Jewish people in the face of the many times misguided Christians made it very costly to courageously remain faithful to God. The God we Christians say we worship is the God of that history as well.

And I was deeply saddened to see the following statement concerning those "who conspired to put Jesus on the cross" in Wright's commentary for "everyone" on 1 Corinthians:

> Judaism, under the rule of the chief priests, in an uneasy relationship with Herod Antipas, "the king of the Jews," played their part by keeping the local people on side with Rome's decision (emphasis mine).[6]

This "Everyone" series serves a wonderful purpose and is well done; yet even here we find this statement that encourages the tendency to see Jesus and his followers as "*not* Judaism," but rather as "Christians" being attacked by "anti-Christian Jews." Such statements reinforce for "everyone" the sad tendency to see the New Testament as anti-Judaism and perhaps anti-Semitic as well. I am quite certain that Wright would say that he did not mean to be heard that way, but the fact that I instantly read it that way almost guarantees that most Jewish people would hear it that way. Sadly, many Christians would hear it that way and nod approvingly.

In historical reality, Jesus and his followers were as much the "Judaism" of their day as were the High Priestly clan members. The many other Jewish people of the time who disliked and distrusted the High Priestly clan at least as intensely as did any writer in the New Testament were also the "Judaism" of that era. So were the "great number of the Jewish priests who became obedient to the faith" (Acts 6:7). So were "the believers who belonged to the sect of the Pharisees" (Acts 15:6), and who after serious debate "consented" as a part of "the whole church" (Acts 15:22) and voted for the "unanimous decision" (Acts 15:25) to send a letter along with

---

5. Wright, Paul and Faithfulness, 1414.

6. Wright, 1 Corinthians Everyone, 25

reputable Jewish representatives to tell the "believers of Gentile origin" that their members were recognized as "brothers." As noted above, Acts 21:20 claims that decades after Jesus's execution there were thousands of "Jews zealous for the law" who were followers of Jesus in Jerusalem. Clearly, these followers of Jesus are a part of first-century "Judaism."

I have no intention of trashing N. T. Wright. As I mentioned, I find him to be a brilliant, thorough, and insightful scholar, to whom I owe a large debt of gratitude. This reality, however, only increases my sadness concerning how difficult it seems for even our best and brightest Christian scholars to escape our ingrained prejudices. Though I, too, have at times tragically failed in this regard, there is no excuse for any of us. We are called to grace, not to prejudice.

How dare we continue to express a supposed Christian superiority when it was "our people" who supported anti-Semitism and anti-Judaism in a manner that led to the Holocaust, which the Jewish artist Marc Chagall aptly portrays as the crucifixion of the Jews in his 1938 painting "White Crucifixion." If Paul, as a follower of Jesus, was busy writing letters to the churches today, I am certain that he would be busy taking Christians to task. I am sure he would find a way to honor the centuries of faithfulness toward God expressed in the lives of many Jewish people whom Christians have both intentionally and unintentionally pushed farther and farther away from the Jewish Jesus. After all, Paul never tired of celebrating his own Jewishness and the Jewishness of the Jesus he followed. As he would, we can, honor centuries of Jewish faithfulness without giving up one whit of his, and our, intense commitment to "the God and Father of our Lord Jesus the Messiah."

6

A Few Practical Pastoral Responses

I HOPE HAVING PROVIDED some of the overall context from which I am writing, and from which I am not writing, helps clarify some of the suggestions that follow. As a pastor, I have spent fifty years wrestling with the relationship between my trust in what God has done through Jesus and better ways to relate to Jews and Judaism. I have learned as much in my failures as in my successes, but hopefully, I have grown in the process. Here are some practical pastoral responses derived from my experiences. These experiences have led me to believe that those of us who wish to follow Jesus more fully must actively practice truth, tears, turning and trusting, in both our attitudes and our behaviors. It is time because it is way past time!

LET'S CONFESS OUR SINS OPENLY AND REGULARLY—TRUTH MUST BE FIRST.

Being truthful is always a good starting place. Bryan Stevenson of *The Just Mercy Initiative* says of the United States exactly what Nelson Mandela earlier maintained in South Africa. If there is no openly confessed truth about past racial injustices, there will be no potential for genuine, deep reconciliation, and without reconciliation the needed healing will not be possible.[7] The same is true about Christian anti-Semitism and anti-Judaism. Pastors (and seminary professors and Christian writers) should regularly confess the truth concerning Christian and Church sins against Jewish people as a part of sermons, books, and teachings.

This open confession should be done, not primarily as an attempt to impress Jewish people, or to ensure ourselves that we are "progressive Christians," but as an attempt to express some level of genuine integrity. Often it will be a very salient application of a text or a point. When it is not central to the teaching, it can still be a "sidebar" comment similar to those most pastors and writers use with other issues we address.

How has it happened that a community based in God's costly act of forgiveness and mercy through Jesus has become a community so reticent to fully acknowledge its failures regarding race, immigration, women, money, power, nationalism, various religions, Jews, and Judaism? I have spent my fifty years as pastor among both conservative and progressive Christians, and we are all culpable. Neither you personally, nor your church, is innocent. Most likely, even your favorite translation of the Bible is not an innocent one when it comes to Christians relating to Jews. For a modern Christian to claim innocence regarding our treatment—past and present—of Jewish people is comparable to a White American Christian claiming innocence when it comes to the sin of racism or a European claiming innocence when it comes to the privileges bestowed by Colonialism. We who are white Americans have all been privileged by systems that have been filled with racist acts and racist words, and we who are Christians have been privileged by systems filled with anti-Semitic and anti-Judaic acts and words.

Truth, Tears, Turning, and Trusting are supposed to be the fabric of the relationship God is offering us. Let's begin telling the truth!

7. Stevenson, Bryan, TED Talk.

LET'S BE CLEAR: "SOME" IS NOT "ALL," AND "THEN" IS NOT "NOW."

Second, we can be very clear that there is no reason to see first-century Jewish synagogue and Temple leaders as any worse than Christian church leaders are now, or have been through the centuries. Perhaps some were not better than some Christian leaders have been, but they were certainly not worse. Without attempting to be too anachronistic, it is helpful for Christians to understand that both the good and the bad Jewish religious leaders described in the New Testament were "church" leaders. "Church" leaders in the sense that *qahal*, the Hebrew for assembly, was translated into the Greek Old Testament (LXX) most often as *ekklesia*—church/assembly, and second most often as *sunagoge*—synagogue/gathering. Synagogue and Temple leaders were Jesus's "church" leaders. This Greek translation soon became the direct source of the New Testament writers' identification of followers of Jesus as "church."

Without ignoring the history that has made "church" a Christian word modern Jews would not apply to themselves; it can be helpful for Christians to see that any criticism of Jewish leaders of their first-century community of faith in the New Testament was a criticism of the "church" leaders of the day. This means it is also a criticism of the "church" leaders of our day.

It is not anti-Semitic or anti-Judaism to entertain the possibility that some of the Pharisees might have been as disgustingly self-righteous as many of the pastors I have known in my life have been—and as I have no doubt that I have been at times. However, it is totally anti-Semitic and anti-Judaic to extrapolate what could have been the actions of only some into a condemnation of all. And, it is a ludicrous, self-serving act of denial to apply critiques of some leaders two millennia ago to Jewish people today, when the only proper application is to our "Christian" selves.

Did some synagogue and temple (church) leaders of Jesus's day steal the resources of widows as Jesus is said to have claimed? I have no reason to doubt that Jesus said it, and that it occurred. However, what I know for sure is that many Christian televangelists in our day have done so, as have several small-town pastors I know of! Christian televangelist Jim Bakker was convicted of 24 counts of fraud and conspiracy in 1989 in his misuse of "God's money." Cardinal McCarrick was found guilty in December 2019 of having misused $600,000 from church funds to bribe Vatican investigators in order to avoid sexual abuse charges, treating those church funds as his own personal pocket money. Caiaphas might have been no better when it came to Temple funds; he cannot have been more corrupt.

I imagine that some of the leaders in the time of Jesus were no better than the high priest during Jeremiah's time, whom Jeremiah blasted without being anti-Semitic, and I am positive that the Jewish leaders in Jeremiah's and in Jesus's time, who were corrupted by political power, were no worse than those popes, cardinals, Protestant theologians, and Protestant pastors who have been blatantly corrupted by the lure of political power, prestige, sexual abuse, and wealth through the centuries—not to mention the current sexual abuses and disastrous political messages of current Protestant, Catholic, and Evangelical church leaders.

Did some ethnically, and perhaps religiously, Jewish people join in "the crowd" that cheered the arrest and crucifixion of Jesus? Not too difficult to imagine, given that we know for certain that thousands of "white Christian" people attended the "legal" lynching of African Americans and Mexican Americans—many of whom were fellow Christians—after they attended Sunday church services. Most of us insist on trying to remind others that this was only "some" white Christians, not all. Why haven't we had the decency to read and teach the New Testament claims within the same grace and mercy we so easily grant ourselves? Even as I write that fully legitimate question, I realize that many American Christians have not been truthful and tearful about widespread support of racism and even lynching by vast sectors of the American church, either. Truth, Tears, Turning, and Trusting really does come hard for us doesn't it?

Pastors, writers, and teachers need to again and again make it clear that the only proper way for a Christian today to read the criticisms in the New Testament of "the scribes and Pharisees" and "the High Priests" and "the Synagogue" and "the Jews" is to see that they speak to us Christians, not to modern Judaism. Written today, these texts would read "Seminary professors," "Christian theologians," "pastors," "popes," "preachers," "denominational leaders," "the church," "Christians," and without question would be especially focused on some very serious and very observant Christians. If we consistently took this step, we would undoubtedly add "some" when we read the New Testament, just as we do when we speak about the current realities in the leadership of churches.

When I preach, I add "some religious leaders," or "the church leaders of the day," or "the church power elite," or "those most insistent on obedience," or "the denominational leadership" in the texts using "the Jews" in order to press this point. I also often stop and remind the listeners that almost every character mentioned in the Gospels is a person we would designate as ethnically Jewish. Of course, in Jesus's environment, the roles that were being critiqued were filled by ethnic "Jews," as we use the term today, but so were all early followers of Jesus, as were all those writers doing the critiquing (except Luke). And, Jesus too was an ethnic Jew! Is this still an inconvenient truth?

LET'S EMPHASIZE THAT CRITIQUING OUR "OWN" IS DIFFERENT FROM CRITIQUING "OTHERS."

Most of us are quite aware that critiques from within a group sound different when the same words are repeated in critiques by outsiders. I do a lot of criticizing of Christians, the church, and America. I do so because I deeply care about each. However, I am often frustrated when similar critiques come from outsiders who show no indication that they are aware of the beautiful side of these communities I care about.

This reality is evident when words used by a family member in an argument with another family member are then repeated by a non-family member in critiquing the same person. Suddenly the sister who criticized her brother changes sides: "You can't say that about my brother." We see the same when a white American repeats the words used by a black American in critiquing certain decisions by other blacks. Suddenly, every word sounds different in the mouth of a white person. In fact, it doesn't just sound different; it is different! Context always matters.

We need to constantly remind modern Christians that words used by first-century Jewish followers of Jesus who were arguing with fellow Jews over who best understood God's purpose in choosing the Jewish people do not sound the same in our mouths today. When we repeat these critiques today, they are no longer words about "us," but rather words about "them." The difference is massive! If we wish to repeat these first-century critiques today, there is only one way to apply them with integrity. Because they were originally in-the-family critiques, we must apply them to Christians, not to Jews. And, we need to make this clear every time we read these parts of the New Testament.

Most first-century Jews expected people like the Roman Pilate to act as nonchalantly and viciously as he did, but what sometimes broke their hearts was when their Jewish leaders acted in a similar manner. Likewise, though it is very sad when the Pilates of our culture act this way, for me as a Christian it is when "our people" who claim to be serious Christians talk and act this way in the name of Jesus that my heart breaks. When these Christians are also prominent and influential leaders, I experience what I think is a justified extra surge of righteous anger and frustration.

Some of us find it important to criticize those we consider "our own" far more passionately than those we see as outside our circle. We should be making it clear in our sermons and Bible studies that the New Testament writers were among those who critiqued their "own" Jewish brothers and sisters more passionately than they critiqued the Romans. Recently in a conversation with a friend, I vehemently criticized what the United States is doing concerning race and immigration. I focused on the United States, even though I know that many other countries are enacting measures that are as bad or worse. Why? Because the United States is my country, and I both want and expect better. I was taught to be proud that we wanted to be the country the Statue of Liberty says we are. I am right to expect us to be better. Let's be clear that this is what the New Testament writers were also doing.

We are following in the footsteps of the Old Testament prophets and the New Testament writers when we criticize what Christians in the United States are doing in the name of God far more vehemently than we criticize the many professional politicians and Wall Street tycoons who make little or no pretense of living out Jesus's values. We are more passionate in critiquing those who claim to be serious Christians, not because they are worse, but because they are "our people" and claim to care deeply about Jesus's values. It is what I see as blatant failure, sometimes blatant hypocrisy, with regard to Jesus's values that makes me so ashamed and angry about what many Christians are doing and saying.

I don't expect any better of those on Wall Street who openly worship the dollar and see "the laws of supply and demand" as more fundamental to reality than the "laws of God." Neither do I expect much "Jesus imaging" from most of the self-centered Congress, which for decades allowed its members to be the only people in the country who could legally use insider information for their investments, and who continue to privilege themselves with gold-standard health care while taking basic care away from others. Of course, they should all be held accountable to the general ethics that are supposed to be the foundation of the U.S. democracy and republic, but I have every right to expect more of people who say they are serious about following Jesus.

When we teach from the New Testament texts that critique some of the Pharisees and most of the High Priestly clan, let's emphasize that these were "their people," and if the accused actually did act as the writers say they did, then the writers were appropriately hurt, disappointed, and frustrated. Then let's immediately reapply the text to the proper roles today, which will be professional Christian leaders. The Romans were brutal occupiers, and everyone knew not to count on them. Every Jewish person knew a Roman governor would brutally execute a Jewish person with little to no concern about guilt—they had seen it before. Roman justice was for Roman citizens. The early followers of Jesus were not stunned when Pilate played political games and knowingly sentenced an innocent man to death. Actually, they were stunned when two or three Roman centurions—out of many—proved to be quite different from what they expected.

However, they were shocked when some of the religious leaders they had respected all their lives as godly people cooperated in the legal charade. They were even stunned that those of the high priestly clan for whom they had much less respect—as did most other Jewish people of the time—stooped so low as to plot to rid the country and the ancient church of a godly Jewish man named Jesus. Just as we should be floored that so many Christian leaders have supported racism throughout U.S. history and are at this very moment justifying the mistreatment of immigrants and refugees. It might be politically understandable, but it is heartbreaking. It was gut-wrenching then, and it is gut-wrenching now.

The only proper application of New Testament passages about Jews is "us," not "them," and "some," not "all." When Christians today read these New Testament texts as though they are a critique of Judaism or of Jews, rather than a critique of some specific leaders in Jesus's time, we are increasing the already voluminous sins of the church against Jewish people.

I would argue that the words of the prophets, the words of Jesus, and the words of the New Testament writers became anti-Semitic and anti-Judaism in the mouths of the Gentile Christian church fathers who used them to reinforce their anti-Semitic (ethnic) and anti-Judaic (religious) prejudices. It was in the writings and preaching of these early church fathers that the critiques of "us" became the critiques of "them." This move changed the original critique from the Jewish prophetic critique of old, which maintained that God's people often failed to enact fully their covenant relationship with God and thus also failed to be God's light to the nations, into Christian bashing of Jewish people as "no longer God's people."

Hosea says God threatens such an action, but could never follow through with it because of God's love for Israel. Like Hosea, Paul refuses to even entertain the possibility of God disinheriting the Jewish people in Romans 9–11: "God forbid" (see especially 11:1–2, 11:26, and 9:4–5). Early Christian leaders, unlike Hosea and Paul, seemed to have no problem envisioning God doing so. They were busy changing the critique from "us" to "them."

In fact, it is often because Jews love Judaism and because Christians love Christianity that they critique their family. I was ashamed and embarrassed beyond words by what Christian leaders and vocal Christian laypersons said and did during the 18 months leading up to the 2016 elections in the United States. I am no less appalled by what many are now doing and saying 18 months after that election.

When Dostoevsky (himself blatantly anti-Semitic) wrote "The Grand Inquisitor" chapter of *The Brothers Karamazov*,[8] he was performing in fiction a scathing critique of the church and church leaders, not because he was anti-Christian, but because he believed that they as church and Christian were anti-Jesus and therefore anti-Christian. Kierkegaard's philosophical critique of the church and its leaders was no less scathing, and it too was because he was pro-Jesus, not because he was anti-Christian. More recently, Martin Luther King Jr.'s critique of the American church was as a pastor and theologian within the church, not as an outsider.

Likewise, our past and present anti-Semitism and anti-Judaism, and our use of some Bible verses to justify it, is inexcusable. The New Testament texts that accuse point at us Christians today, not at Jewish people.

One further thought on this "us" versus "them" application of New Testament words. The word "Jew" (*Ioudaioi* in koine Greek) seems to have had many definitions, not just a broad ethnic usage. In Jesus's day, the leadership roles were often filled by "the Jews," not so much corresponding to either our current ethnic or religious sense of the term, but in the more restricted senses that sometimes identified the first-century Jerusalem elite, political, economic, religious leaders, and sometimes the more observant Jews of the time. Josephus (*Antiquities* XVIII, 2) seems to have occasionally used the term "Jew" in this manner as well. Using the more "observant" sense of the word, Paul identifies Peter, Barnabas, and himself as still belonging to the "Jews" in Galatians 2:14–15, even though they

---

8. Dostoevsky, Karamazov, 127–137.

had been followers of Jesus for several years. This coincides with the New Testament usage of "Jews" sometimes limited to those similar to "the Pharisees"—see Mark 7:3, for example, where "all the Jews" is in contrast with the ethnically Jewish disciples and with many other ethnic Jews of the time who did not practice the daily ceremonial washings prescribed by the Pharisees.

Of course, all the non-Roman first-century power brokers in Israel of Jesus's time were ethnically Jewish, but the term seems to sometimes be used much more restrictively to identify people with religious, political, and/or economic power. The use of "the Jews" in John 18 is a great example of the conundrum that faces us. Throughout this chapter the term seems not to refer to the many different views of various ethnic "Jews," but to an inner circle of power brokers who were identified as "the Jews."

This linguistic issue is not as strange as it might seem at first blush. Modern examples of using group identity words in a similar way include how many of us Americans talk about "Washington," when we mean only the powerbrokers, not the millions of largely disenfranchised citizens who live in Washington DC. Or, you might think of the way the rest of the world says "the Americans did. . . . " or "the Russians did. . . . " or "the Chinese did. . . ." meaning not the people of America or Russia or China, but the elite leaders. And, for further insight, you might think about how easily we then forget what we have done when we use such language, and do in fact start thinking of all Russians or all Chinese as being like their leaders. Ironically, all the while hoping that the rest of the world does not blame all Americans for some of the horrible decisions made by our leaders.

So yes, if you take the claims as historically serious, the New Testament writers were criticizing some leaders who were ethnically "Jewish" and identifying themselves as "Jewish" by faith as well. Just as obviously, when today we apply the New Testament critiques to the American church, or to the churches of the world, the vast majority of equivalent roles are filled by people who self-identify as "Christians," and these "Christians" often make some of us ashamed, heart-broken, angry, and very frustrated.

LET'S STRESS THAT NEW TESTAMENT WRITERS WERE ALREADY REFOCUSING THEIR CRITIQUES ON FOLLOWERS OF JESUS.

Another practical step toward combating the use of the New Testament as a tool for anti-Semitism is to stress that the same critiques that are made in various New Testament writings of some of the Jewish leaders were also already being applied to some "Christian" (our word, not theirs) leaders by New Testament writers. Both 1 and 2 Corinthians include scathing critiques of church leaders. 1 John calls some apparently Gentile church leaders "anti-Christs" or "anti-Messiahs." Galatians says some of the Christian leaders should just go ahead and castrate themselves, and others should be "accursed" for preaching a different good news. The author of 2 Peter says Christian leaders (again apparently Gentile) are exploiting women sexually and are more concerned about money than truth. Jude, 3 John, James, 1 and 2 Timothy, and Revelation report their shame and anger concerning the teachings and actions of Christian church leaders.

Followers of Jesus have no excuse for reading the New Testament critiques of some Jewish leaders as God's rejection of the Jews while reading the same critiques of some early Christian church leaders without even entertaining the thought that God is rejecting "Christianity" or rejecting "the early Jesus Movement." When the critique is of "us," we quickly add "some" to the critique, whether we are thinking of "our" first century leaders or "our" current leaders and churches. So much grace for ourselves and so little for others! On what basis?

LET'S ACKNOWLEDGE THAT HISTORICAL APPLICATION OFTEN TRUMPS ORIGINAL INTENT.

However, to be practical, we must practice truth-telling. Even those of us pastors and teachers who think the New Testament writers themselves were innocent with regard to anti-Semitism and anti-Judaism must be clear that their original intent has not been a primary shaper of Western culture or of church history. The way these texts were read by church leaders in the following centuries has been determinative of most church history regarding the Jewish people. As Christians, our own perverted ways of relating to Jewish people through the centuries have created a situation in which every New Testament text that says something negative about some Jewish people at a given moment in history will today be heard by every Jewish person, and by the large majority of Christians, as anti-Judaism and probably as anti-Semitic.

This means that not one of these texts can be read or written today as though it were an "innocent" statement. Because we Christians cannot escape these texts—they are in our Bible—when we do need to use them, we must stop and respond to the way they are now heard. A pastor or teacher should never allow one of these texts to either stand alone or to be read without additional comments.

I recently found it necessary to preach another sermon pleading for the church community I participate in not to forget this important responsibility. Our current pastor is deeply committed to honoring our Jewish neighbors. As pastor I was, and as pastor emeritus I am, deeply committed to this goal. Still, both she and I find it important to stress our concern regularly because we swim against a stream of deeply embedded anti-Semitic and anti-Judaic theology and Biblical interpretation that is centuries old. These understandings are in the water we drink, even in a community that is dedicated to the inclusiveness of "Jesus's open table."

WE MUST BE SURE OUR "REPENTANCE" IS GENUINE; NOT CONDESCENDING AND SELF-AGGRANDIZING.

Another practical thing pastors and teachers can do when we attempt to recontextualize New Testament texts is to be certain we do not speak condescendingly, as though we Christians were trying to "be nice" about a problem Jewish people have with "our" texts. Christians all over the world are hearing and using these texts in anti-Semitic and anti-Judaic ways at this very hour. Of course, this causes problems for Jewish people worldwide. However, this is also a major Christian problem in exactly the same way that the misuse of texts on slavery, homosexuality, patriarchy, and race have been a problem that needs confession and repentance by Christians—we have been the oppressors. It is not only the oppressed, but also the oppressors, whose lives are scarred when we use our texts to justify oppression.

When we fail to be sensitive to how a text we use will be heard, and we will fail, we need to circle back and acknowledge our failure. Often apparent attempts by Christians to repent for our failures of the past turn out to sound more like excuses than repentance.

At this point, I want to step onto ground where in many ways no Christian has a right to go. The *Holocaust*, the vicious destruction of more than six million Jews, plus millions of other human lives, is a raw evil of such proportions that it overwhelms the mind and heart. Historically, it was a horrific failure on the part of many nations, and tragically, on the part of most Christians around the world. We Christians have little or no right to speak about it to Jewish people; listening with tears rather than speaking should be our primary response.

On the other hand, if we Christians do not speak of it with one another, we stand in danger of repeating such horrific sins again. Even much of our repentance has tended to continue to be more sinful than repentant. In fact, what begins as though it is going to be a time of repentance, often ends up focusing on the few Christians who did well, rather than the many who failed miserably. No Jewish person misses the irony when our repentance for the Holocaust turns out to primarily aggrandize the few—very few—Christian heroes. I certainly honor the courage of the Ten Boom family, the villagers of Le Chambon, and Father Josef Gorajek, each of whom risked their lives to save Jewish people. I am deeply challenged by their risky faithfulness; however, we must not forget to be clear that they were among the comparatively few Christians who took these risks.

Our lack of real confession, lamentation, and repentance becomes painfully obvious when Christians speak mainly of the

Holocaust in terms of the few Christians who were martyred because they helped Jewish people and risked opposing the Nazis, while we barely, if at all, acknowledge that millions of Christians, and thousands of Christian leaders, in Germany and world-wide, never opposed, and often supported, the abuse of the Jews. Perhaps our real concern becomes most obvious when Father Kolbe, who gave his life to save a Polish soldier—impressive to say the least—becomes the canonized church hero at Auschwitz, with no note of how many Jews he did not offer his life in place of and with no equal honoring of Father Gorajek who did risk his life to save Jewish people.[9]

I appreciate and honor the few heroes who were Christians, but that is not the primary reality of the Holocaust. Our horrendous failure as people who claim to follow Jesus is the main narrative, and heart-deep repentance and lament should be our current focus. Our continuing failure to "tell it like it was" becomes a part of our continuing denial of our anti-Semitism and anti-Judaism—our ongoing failure to "tell it like it is."

In contrast, I watched my pastor recently be genuinely confessional and repentant. No excuses! Truth, Tears, Turning, and Trusting, after the front of the church bulletin in my church fellowship featured the following text:

> [1]At Iconium Paul and Barnabas went as usual into the Jewish synagogue. There they spoke so effectively that a great number of Jews and Gentiles believed. [2]But the Jews who refused to believe stirred up the Gentiles and poisoned their minds against the brothers. [3]So Paul and Barnabas spent considerable time there, speaking boldly for the Lord, who confirmed the message of his grace by enabling them to do miraculous signs and wonders. [4]The people of the city were divided; some sided with the Jews, others with the apostles. (Acts 14:1–4.)

Regardless of how texts like this were meant in the first century, when followers of Jesus saw themselves as the oppressed minority, today after centuries of the church oppressing Jews, left to stand alone, these texts are often heard as anti-Semitic and anti-Judaism.

9. Carroll, Constantine's Sword, 3–5.

However, most of us, probably all of us who are not ethnically Jewish, will forget at times and will let texts like this stand alone in a liturgy, a classroom, or a sermon. Instead, we should imitate what our wonderful pastor did in her blog to the congregation two days later. We can confess, repent, and ask for forgiveness for perpetuating the sins of our forefathers—no excuses. Here are a few of her words of public truth, tears, and turning:

> I speak as someone who just completely missed it. Someone who printed a piece of scripture on the bulletin cover that would only later be contextualized. The painful irony was that the message reminded us of the danger of Luther's anti-Semitism, while the text of Acts 14:1–4 reinforced the division that led to that very hatred. How did that happen? It happens because each of us has blind spots. (Renée Antrosio. Used by permission.)

Truth, Tears, Turning, and Trusting, in the words and actions of a humble and humbled woman!

LET'S NOTE REGULARLY THAT ALMOST EVERY CHARACTER IN THE NEW TESTAMENT IS "JEWISH," AS WE USE THE TERM ETHNICALLY TODAY.

We can also regularly include in sermons and in public statements explanations that all the apostles, and probably all but one of the writers of the New Testament, were proudly "Jewish." Some of them did occasionally use the word translated "Jew" in a negative sense, but when they did so, it did not mean what it means in our ears today. Before I retired from preaching regularly, I would periodically decide that I had made comments like what I just wrote so often that they were no longer needed. Invariably, a conversation within the next week or two would make it clear to me that they will unfortunately be needed for a long time to come.

It is important that we regularly acknowledge in sermons and classrooms how terrible Christians have been in applying "fulfillment" passages as well as in failing to contextualize New Testament statements about "Jews." Addressing this issue later in the book, I will acknowledge that the New Testament claims of fulfillment will always create tension between Christians and Jews. However, the way fulfillment has come to be understood and taught through the centuries by Christians is another example of how the original textual intent in its historical context differs dramatically from the way we hear these passages in the modern context we Christians have helped to create. The original Jewish authors certainly did not think fulfillment meant that God was discarding the Jews, because they continued to self-identify as Jews.

LET'S REMIND PEOPLE WHY SOME CAME TO SEE JESUS AS A THREAT.

We need to remind our listeners that those who saw Jesus as a threat did so for the same reason people see other people as a threat today. It is rarely really about someone's doctrinal beliefs. We may vehemently disagree with what someone says she or he believes, but it is when actions start to become seen as a threat to national or church institutional stability and security that leaders start to react powerfully to what you believe about God.

Powerful people did not care very much what the early Anabaptists, or the Protestant reformers, or Martin Luther King Jr. believed doctrinally—until they began to act on what they believed in ways that were seen as destabilizing and threatening to the institutions and their power brokers. As I mentioned earlier, most historians agree that a man named Jesus was executed in first-century Jerusalem, which was the power center of first century Judaism. Does this mean most Jewish people wanted this man Jesus dead? No! Of course not!

Most Jewish people of the day would have known less, not more, about what their leaders were doing than most of us today know about what is going on behind the scenes in the White House, the Pentagon, or the Congress. Truthfully, we don't know very much either, do we? I just listened to half an hour of "news" in which the correspondents all attempted to guess at what was going on in the White House at this moment. It was clear they didn't really know much, even though they spend their days trying to find out. The rest of us "common everyday" Americans obviously know less about what is going on. Why not grant the same reality to the "common everyday" Jewish person of Jesus's time?

Current Democrat and Republican leaders are constantly claiming to speak for and represent "the American people," while they act behind the scenes for reasons most American people know little about. Often, when I find out what they are really doing, it is clear to me that, whoever they think "the American people" are, on behalf of whom they claim to be speaking, it does not include most of the American people I know.

Similarly, some Jewish leaders might have cooperated with Rome to get Jesus crucified and might have claimed to speak for "the Jews." This did not occur because most Jewish people agreed; most Jewish people didn't even know what was happening behind the scenes. Many would have been horrified, had they known what was going on behind closed doors, no matter what they thought about Jesus's Messiahship, just as many of us today, regardless of our political affiliations, would be horrified at what goes on behind closed doors in the White House, the Senate, the Congress, the Supreme Court, and the Pentagon.

The majority of Americans or American Christians know that these leaders often are not speaking for "the American people" when they claim they are; just as the majority of first-century Jews would have known that the leaders did not truly speak for the Jewish People. They would also have known that Jesus was not really executed because of what Jesus thought about God, but because Jesus's beliefs about God were being enacted in ways that were seen by powerful people as dangerous to the status quo. Jesus was seen by enough political and religious leaders as a potential threat to the stability of the structures that sustained their personal realms of power, money, pride, and prestige that he needed to be stopped. Most of the Jewish people would have had little knowledge or power in the situation. Apparently, according to the Gospel writers, their leaders then, like ours today, often pretended to speak for "all the people"—meaning all the people whose opinion they cared about.

For most Jewish people, the actions of the High Priestly clan headed by Annas and Caiaphas would have no more represented "the Jews" than did the crucifixion in 88 BC of about 800 Pharisees by the Jewish High Priest and King Alexander Jannaeus. He, too, claimed he did it for the good of the Jewish people, but it is not difficult to see that the later evaluations by Jewish teachers and historians, who were mostly Pharisees, maintaining that he crucified these fellow Jews in an attempt to protect his power, wealth, and prestige, ring far truer than the sympathetic evaluations by his Sadducean supporters.

It has been for exactly these same reasons that so many Christian leaders down through the centuries, and today, have cooperated in destroying both fellow Christians and other people whom they have seen as threats to their personal power, money, and prestige—their security and stability. Many Christian leaders of 1960s America belittled Martin Luther King Jr. as a communist and traitor, as a way of hiding from others—and often from themselves—how deeply they resented the fact that MLK's Christian values exposed their racism and their white privilege.

Religious institutional leaders and political Empire leaders usually care very little when you critique your own religious circles and your own religious leaders, unless they begin to fear that your critiques are starting to impinge on the stability and security of their personal power, money, and prestige, which they are convinced is "for the good of all the people," or at least they are convinced that you need to think it is "for the good of all the people."

It is dishonest and filled with anti-Judaic prejudice to speak of the encounters between Jesus and some Jewish leaders of his time as though the primary issue were Jewish religious legalism, or as though "the Jews killed Jesus" because he was the first Christian preacher. If we take the accounts in the Gospels seriously, the primary tensions were, as they always are, around institutional and national security and stability, as it was interpreted by those in power. And then, as now, leaders might have claimed to act on behalf of "the people," and then, as now, they might well have been able to gather a relatively large cheering crowd to support their actions and jeer their enemies; but the truth then and now is that most of "the people" have little power, little say, and little knowledge about what is really going on behind the scenes. Then and now, even those in the cheering crowd gathered for political PR purposes usually represent only a minority and rarely know how they are being manipulated and used.

As for the Roman Empire, they crucified thousands of Jews as an expression of their understanding of the security and stability of the Empire and its Pax Romana (Roman Peace). In fact, historians note that Jesus would have grown up in a town that had experienced more than 2,000 Jewish males from the area being crucified by the Romans not long before Jesus was born. Because no one would turn in a small band of "terrorists," Rome randomly rounded up 2,000 men to execute as a clear sign of who was in charge—massive random retaliatory terror to deal with terrorists. They then crucified them all along the roadways in order to terrorize the Galileans and to make it clear who was in charge. It made no difference to the Romans whether any of the 2,000 tortured and executed were guilty or not.

This event was probably viewed by the Romans very much as many Americans viewed the retaliatory bombing of Iraq because of the horrible destruction of the twin towers. It didn't really matter that no Iraqis had been involved, or that the horrific attacks had been carried out by predominantly Saudi terrorists. We wanted all the Middle East to know that we were in control, and we would not stand for anything that appeared to destabilize that political and economic control. Just as we can be sure that the retelling of this event sounds quite different in the millions of bombed out homes of Iraqis, we can be sure that the retelling of the "we'll show them" event of random retaliatory executions was rampant in the streets and homes of Nazareth for decades to come. Like every Jew who was perceived to in any way threaten the stability of Roman rule, Jesus would have had no doubt what the outcome would likely be, as he began to be viewed as a threat. He knew that in the name of peace, justice, and law-and-order, he would be swatted off like a bothersome fly.

Roman political and military leaders did not care how many gods you worshipped—unless somehow your faith in God began to cause actions that rattled political policy. Pilate's responses to Jesus in the Gospels indicate that he did not really care whether Jesus was guilty or innocent of being a danger to Rome, but history indicates that he did care about looking good before the Emperor with whom he was already on thin ice because his earlier brutality toward Jews had already destabilized the province. So, he acquiesces to those Jewish leaders who see Jesus as a populist troublemaker who poses a danger to their security and power. "Roman justice" in this instance is a decision that has nothing to do with God, and nothing to do with guilt as an insurrectionist against Rome, but is entirely a military and political "peace-keeping" act. The response of the Roman proconsul Gallio in Acts 18:14–15 makes this same Roman policy very clear, when he says he has no interest in religious arguments, but intends to have no one upsetting the political, economic, social status quo of the province he rules.

Whether the church's institutional system or the Empire's institutional system is threatened, the response has almost never been about God or true doctrine. It has almost always been about security and stability—about power, money, and prestige.

The same is true today in America. You will not get in trouble with political leaders or religious leaders for criticizing your church or your denomination—unless your criticisms begin to threaten what leaders perceive as economic stability, institutional stability, national security, or egos and prestige. To illustrate my point—no one in politics cared what Evangelical and Fundamentalist Christians taught or believed during the decades prior to the time when leaders of these groups began to change their approach from "hands off" to "let's take over as the 'moral majority'" in American politics. Now everyone in politics cares—and it has very little to do with God or religious beliefs, but everything to do with power, money, and prestige.

To summarize: Jesus was not executed because he was starting something called "Christianity" that was designed to replace Judaism. Jesus-the-Jew was executed because a powerful Roman governor and the powerful high priestly clan of Annas and Caiaphas agreed that he was a threat to *Pax Romana* and to the power and money of those who ran the Temple. Some Herodians and some Pharisees joined in for their own reasons, but only Pilate and Caiaphas could have made it happen, and they would have made it happen only if they saw Jesus's words and actions as a threat to their institutional power and prestige.

LET'S HAVE THE COURAGE TO SPEAK UP AND ENCOURAGE OTHERS TO DO SO AS WELL.

Yet another practical response we church leaders can make is to have the courage to speak up in our churches and in our society when we hear statements or see actions that are intentionally or unintentionally anti-Semitic or anti-Judaism. In some situations, this takes a good bit of courage and sometimes extra attentiveness to what is actually being said or implied. Just as with racism, sexism, classism, and other prejudices, words or actions that are anti-Semitic or anti-Judaism need to be called out in as helpful a manner as possible.

Courage and wisdom are particularly called for when the anti-Semitism is somewhat covert and implicit rather than open and acknowledged, just as is the case with covert and implicit racist white supremacy or implicit class arrogance. This type of anti-Semitism is often immediately denied, and you are attacked as being unfair and as being trying to be "politically correct."

It is also true that it is wiser and more helpful to speak of words that are anti-Semitic or actions that are anti-Semitic rather than to label persons as anti-Semitic. This allows the person we are confronting to focus on the words or actions if he or she is willing to do so, rather than needing to defend his or her entire identity. As a side benefit, it forces you and me to deal with our own specific failures, rather than to hide behind our "I would never be anti-Semitic" self-identification. As I have said several times, but wish to reiterate, there are no innocent Christians in this area.

WE NEED TO READ AND LISTEN TO
JEWISH AUTHORS AND FRIENDS.

Those of us who are pastors and teachers in churches and seminaries can read, and encourage others to read, Jewish authors, with an honest listening ear and empathy for what they are wrestling with. We can work to become trustworthy enough in our relationships that rabbis and Jewish friends can risk openly talking to us about our failures, their faith, their concerns about Christian evangelism, and their concerns about Christian privilege in our culture.

This openness should include our willingness to be confronted with what are currently being described as microaggressions that people of minority groups bring to the attention of those of us who are in the majority. Actually, I agree with Ibram X. Kendi, who maintains that what are currently being called "microaggressions" should be identified as "abuse" because they truly do add up to a treacherous form of abusiveness.[10] To call them "micro" is to belittle their true impact on those who are abused. Usually these are insults and prejudices that, in the past, we have not been willing to identify in our own words and actions, and do not consider as being as belittling as they are. Almost always, we are tempted to rebut and declare our good intentions. We need to learn instead to listen to those who experience our words and actions as abuse and to reflect carefully on their responses.

GOD'S CONTINUING HISTORY WITH JUDAISM
VERIFIES "REPLACEMENT" IS FALSE.

In the next two chapters, I will illustrate that New Testament authors did not think that their claims of "fulfillment" meant "replacement" or "rejection" of Jews and Judaism. Here, I want to note a related practical step we can take that is far less complicated.

We can combat anti-Semitism and anti-Judaism by insisting that both the Old Testament and the New Testament strongly declare that God is the God of real history, and history is another reason

10. Kendi, Anti-Racist.

fulfillment in Jesus should not be seen by twenty-first-century followers of Jesus as intended to be the end of Judaism. God certainly has not abandoned the Jews, and faithful Jewish people have certainly not abandoned God. That historical reality says something powerful about God and about Jewish faithfulness to God.

History since the time of Jesus is replete with both heroic faithfulness and more *ordinary* faithfulness in the lives of many Jewish people. If the God described in the New Testament is real, then there is every reason for followers of Jesus to honor the very real continuing historical developments since Jesus's time. God's hand has clearly been positively at work in sustaining Judaism and the Jewish people throughout the last two millennia. This is seen in the survival of the Jewish people, despite the sins of Christians (and of others) toward them.

Genuine faithfulness is also easy to see in the deep, spiritual relationship with God exhibited by Jewish writers, such as the scholarly books of Abraham Joshua Heschel (e.g., *God in Search of Man*) or the more devotional books of Rachel Naomi Remen (e.g., *My Grandfather's Blessings: Stories of Strength, Refuge, and Belonging*), and a Christian has to be willfully blind not to see the depths of faithfulness vividly illustrated by the many Jewish faithful who lived and died praying the Shema during the Holocaust:

> [4]Hear, O Israel: The LORD our God, the LORD is one.
> [5]Love the LORD your God with all your heart and with
> all your soul and with all your strength. (Deut 6:4–5.)

These Jewish people died with that prayer on their lips—I can only barely make myself write the following words—while many calling themselves "Christian" turned on the gas valves, drove the death trains, and supported or ignored what was occurring in the streets and shops of their towns.

Russian Communist persecution also brought out a shared faithfulness between Christians and Jews. There are quite a few stories that emanated from Russian Siberian prisons involving Jews and Christians who prayed and supported one another as "brothers and sisters" in clandestine cells of shared faith and faithfulness. Isn't it fascinating how shared suffering and difficult times can bring about a spiritual oneness that we seem to resist in the easier times? Let's not wait for the next widespread persecution that involves both Christians and Jews to find out that we pray to the same God and derive our roots from the same Old Testament.

Surely, we who follow Jesus can acknowledge the obvious acts of God in history without undermining the New Testament understanding of fulfillment. After all, our entire self-understanding flows from the "come and see" claims in the New Testament writings concerning a God who works in real world history. Let's be a people of history as we claim we are and get busy thanking God for sustaining our Jewish brothers and sisters despite the sins of the church (and many others) against them.

SUMMARY

You may well be able to add other practical responses that followers of Jesus should regularly be making to the rampant anti-Semitism and anti-Judaism that still infect our churches. I encourage you to see this as a major concern that needs far more attention than we have tended to give it. We do not just need a better theory; we need much better intentional practices if we are to honor the Jewish Jesus we say we follow.

7

Fulfillment Was Never Meant to Be Replacement.

Fulfillment Is Not Supersession.

IN THIS CHAPTER AND the next, I want to point out that the New Testament writers did not view their claims of fulfillment as replacement or supersession—God's choice of Christians in the place of Jews. Once the move from fulfillment to supersession was made by the "early church fathers," the complete separation between Church and Judaism was inevitable. When those who have moved into your house obtain your eviction notice, there is no room left for table fellowship.

Nothing I am writing is an attempt to deny the obvious fact that fulfillment as it is presented in the pages of the New Testament will always cause a level of unavoidable tension between Christians and Jews. I do believe, however, that there is value for both Christians and Jews in separating out the tensions that flow from the New Testament from those that came into being later as the New Testament was misused to promote the anti-Semitic and anti-Judaic views of later Christians.

One part of this process is recognizing that claiming that Jesus was the Messiah did not automatically guarantee that someone in the first century must choose between being Jewish and following

Jesus as Messiah. There were several people proclaimed as "Messiah" by various Jewish people during the first century BC and the first century AD. This historical reality includes the recognition of Bar Kokhba by the esteemed Rabbi Akiba as late as 132 AD. The tension between those who believed and those who did not believe one of these several Messiahs to genuinely be God's Messiah could and did take place within Judaism. However, once the church defined fulfillment as the church "replacing" Judaism, there was no possibility of that kind of continuing interaction between Jewish people. The impact of that move continues.

Clearly, ascertaining original intent does not correct centuries of abuse. Still, understanding the first-century issues can help us to understand one another better and to empathize more fully with each another.

Once again, I ask that the reader not allow my views of Scripture to become an excuse for avoiding the plea of this book. Many scholars believe that a lot of the words or actions attributed to Jesus in the Gospels are inventions of the authors, read back into their descriptions of Jesus. I certainly recognize the impact of the authors' interests, concerns, communities, and personalities, but I trust, for reasons I find compelling, that the records reflect Jesus's words and actions relatively well.

To pursue the issues surrounding how reliable or unreliable the historical claims of the New Testament are would demand another book—a book added to the hundreds already written on the topic. Even my statement that I think the Gospels reflect the real Jesus in action demands a caveat acknowledging that the Gospel of John contains a lot of later commentary read back into the accounts. In many ways, it reflects the way the author of 1 and 2 Chronicles narrated the history also recorded in 1 and 2 Samuel and 1 and 2 Kings. Richard Bauckham argues that most of the first-century Gentile world thought John's way of doing history was the best way to write history.[11] On the other hand, many of us today prefer the way Mark, Luke, and Matthew present their historical claims, just as we prefer the way 1 and 2 Samuel narrate historical claims. Yet,

11. Bauckham, Eyewitnesses, 8–10.

even in the records many of us today prefer, we see the impact of each author's concerns, sources, and personality.

Whether you believe the various quotations below reflect the original teachings of Jesus, or you think they primarily reflect the viewpoints of later authors, either way they became the source of many of the later tensions between Jews and Christians. My goal in this chapter and the next is to show that some of that tension came, not from Jesus or the New Testament writers, but from later anti-Semitism in church interpretation; however, it seems important to first acknowledge clearly some of the unavoidable tensions that will still remain.

FULFILLMENT WILL ALWAYS BE A STICKY ISSUE FOR CHRISTIANS AND JEWS.

I agree with James Carroll when he points out that the New Testament theme of fulfillment has very often been used by Christians to denigrate the Old Testament, as well as to denigrate Judaism in a manner that has encouraged anti-Semitism and supersessionism—the claim that God replaced Jews with Christians and cast Jews away from God's presence and purposes. The resulting history is very ugly and must be acknowledged. However, I disagree with him that supersessionism is inherent in the New Testament understanding of Jesus as God's overflowing fulfillment of God's covenant relationship with humans and with Israel.

Still, I need to acknowledge that the fulfillment theme will always make discussions between Jews and Christians difficult. There is no valid way on either side to avoid the tension that this central New Testament claim causes. It was what the first-century Jewish followers of Jesus as Messiah, and many of the first-century Jewish leaders who did not think Jesus was God's Messiah, never resolved between one another. It is easy to imagine Paul saying to his fellow Pharisees, "Can't you see! It is plain: this is what God has been moving toward all along. This is why we exist as a people!" It is just as easy to hear his peers saying to Paul, "Can't you see! What you are pushing could destroy our culture, our temple, our calling to be Jews who observe the Torah, and maybe even our existence."

I think it is important to recapture some of what was at stake in the first century AD for those on each side of this argument, and then to see that many of the same issues remain today, along with the addition of 1,900 years of Christian anti-Semitism and anti-Judaism added to the mix.

Not surprisingly, the tension created when followers of Jesus speak of him as God's fulfillment of God's covenant promise to Abraham, and the response of some Jewish people today, are just as strong as they were in the first century. From the point of view of a Jewish scholar, Daniel Boyarin describes why the tension will always be there no matter how hard we work at understanding one another.[12] N. T. Wright does the same from the point of view of a Christian scholar.[13] Both Boyarin and Wright do amazing scholarship. Both see Jesus (and Paul) as thoroughly immersed in the first-century Jewish world, and they both make it clear why Jesus and his followers created tension with many other Jews then—and now.

The thoughts that follow are not an attempt to present a solution to the tension these disagreements create. The tension will always be there; however, I do think Christians and Jews can address them more meaningfully and empathetically with one another than we often do.

History has validated the concern of first-century Jewish people who thought that a widespread success of the "Jesus Movement" threatened all of the hard work and success Hellenistic Jews had experienced in incorporating Gentile "God-fearers" and Gentile converts into synagogue worship. History has also borne out the apprehension of those early Jewish leaders who were concerned that a widespread joining of the Jesus movement by Jewish people could become devastating to Jewish community boundaries, Jewish culture, and Jewish practices of Torah-keeping. What Christians have done when they have come to dominate cultures makes it quite clear that these first-century Jewish concerns were not unfounded,

---

12. Boyarin, Radical Jew, 32, 118, 142.

13. Wright, Paul and Faithfulness, 1408–1472

and modern history makes it equally clear that modern Jews who have the same concerns have them for well-founded reasons as well.

When you add to these concerns the fact that Christians claim to be "the fulfillment" of ancient Israel's calling, this by its very nature smacks of the claim, "You Jews are now practicing a second-rate faith"—or worse. It is no wonder that the feeling of being insulted and perhaps threatened by many Christians comes quickly for many Jewish people. How could it not?

On the other hand, giving up the idea of fulfillment means that I, as a Gentile, have based my entire life on a completely false claim that God decided to "bless all nations" by incorporating people like me into the "people of Abraham," through Jesus the Jewish Messiah. I hear the claim by many Jewish people that Jesus was not the fulfillment of the Old Testament promises as maintaining that everything I base my life on is either a mistake or a lie. I hear the claim that fulfillment is not true as a clear statement that "Christianity" is based on a perversion of Judaism, and we are the practitioners of a second-rate—or worse—faith. I hear the claim that my friend cannot really be a Jew and a follower of Jesus as a denial that the Jesus I follow really is God's gift to all peoples of all nations and ethnicities—a denial that Jesus is really alive and active in the world. All these things leave me feeling frustrated and misunderstood. How could I not be?

Certainly, in almost every area of life that matters to us humans, we all think that what we believe to be true is "the right view," and the way we do things is the "better way." Whether we voice it or not, we can hardly help thinking this way. If I vote Republican, I probably think what the Republicans are promising is closer to "right" and is the "better" way forward. If I vote Democrat, I likely think what the Democrats are promising is closer to "right" and is the "better" way forward. If I claim to be an Independent, it probably means either I don't like either of them very much, or I don't care very much. Most people even think that the car they buy is the "best" car at the price they are willing to pay. When we say, "one is as good as another," we almost always mean "this does not matter very much to me," or, "in the big picture of things, this is not that important."

Jews and Christians cannot escape this "our way is better" reality. Even when we say, "better for me," we do not really escape the implication that it might also be "better for you to recognize the weaknesses in your claim." Where Jews and Christians are concerned, this almost inescapable human reality causes an unavoidable tension. This turns out to be somewhat true even for Jews and Christians who do not think the ancient claims about God's actions in real space and time are true.

However, the tension is even more unavoidable for those of us who think that what we believe to be true is rooted in real human history and in genuine interactions between a real and active God and real humans in the real world. If, as Jews and Christians, we think the covenant with Abraham and the Exodus were God's work in real history to create Israel, and if, as followers of Jesus, we think the execution of Jesus truly led to God's saving Jesus from death through resurrection as the beginning of a new step in fulfilling the covenant with Abraham, our actions and our words will show it. Believing that God really acted in these ways in history will at times leave us in unavoidable tension with one another.

Because I am a person who trusts that the ancient texts point us to events that really did occur because of God's relationship with humans, I see no way to fully relieve this built-in tension. On the other hand, I am certain that there are ways for followers of Jesus who are certain Jesus lives as God's Messiah, and for Jewish people who are certain that Jesus and his followers were, and are, mistaken in their understanding of reality, truth, and Judaism, to be more supportive of one another.

One of my personal steps in attempting to do this is writing this book. The local Rabbi who honored me by reading and commenting on an early draft of this book articulated one of his many personal steps in these words:

> To offer just my personal worldview, Judaism is right for me and my family. It is our truth, but it does not negate your truth or your right to hold to it. I feel entirely fulfilled by my faith, while acknowledging that acceptance of Jesus as messiah is central to your sense of fulfillment. Sure, empirically, that's a contradiction. But in the

interest of "shalom" and not being a jerk to my neighbors, it's a contradiction I'm comfortable confronting.
(Used by permission.)

As is probably clear throughout this book, I cannot say exactly the
same words back to him. But with my whole heart I can be thrilled
with his good-heartedness, appreciate him, honor his faith, and
delight in his goodness, as I pray for God to continue to bless him
richly now and to graciously allow us both to share in God's great
future for humans. In response, I can and do also pray that God
will help me be equally good-hearted and gracious toward him and
those he represents.

Will his good intentions and my good intentions do away with
all the tension? Probably not. Is this a step we can both honor in one
another? It seems to be true that we can.

BEFORE AND AFTER JESUS IN
THE NEW TESTAMENT IS NOT
CHRISTIANS REPLACING JEWS.

Fulfillment is a Key New Testament
Theme; Supersession is Not.

Even though the fulfillment theme will still always be a sticking
point between Jews and Christians, those of us who follow Jesus
can at least learn to distinguish both theologically and historically
between fulfillment of patterns and "supersessionism" (Christians
and Christianity replacing Jews and Judaism).

It is true that the New Testament presents a before and after
paradigm for understanding what God has done through God's relationship with Jesus. The before is not, however, a rejection of the
Torah, but a claim that God has used it to bring history to an important next step. In fact, Jesus summarized Torah in exactly the same
manner that some of the other teachers and Bible scholars of his day
were summarizing Torah, by bringing together Deuteronomy 6:4–5
with Leviticus 19:18 (see Mark 12:29–33 and Luke 10:27–28).

Still, the *before* claim in the New Testament is real, and it is a claim that God has moved history forward again through God's covenant relationship with Jesus, just as God earlier moved history forward through God's covenant relationship with Abraham. Apart from that paradigm, the New Testament makes no sense, and neither does the ongoing existence of Christianity. I have no problem seeing why many first-century Jewish people, and many twenty-first-century Jewish people, see this as a major frustration in any attempt to pursue dialogue with Christians.

However, in my opinion it is disingenuous to attempt to dissolve the tension, as several modern Christian scholars do, by denigrating the New Testament claim that through God's relationship with Jesus, God has taken a step forward in self-revelation—a step fully interconnected to God's covenant relationship with Abraham. This claim is essential to the entire New Testament message. Attempts to reconcile Christianity with Judaism by jettisoning the fulfillment theme as writers James Carroll and Bishop Spong do seem to me to be dishonest. If the Jesus who lived, died, and was raised from death in first-century Israel is not a fulfillment of God's prior promises and patterns of revelation, we should totally disavow the New Testament as a completely dishonest religious myth and we should abandon any form of "Christianity" that implies following Jesus.

It can be honest to respond to the New Testament fulfillment claims in various ways such as "I trust them," "I do not trust them at all," "I am not sure what to do with them," or "This is ridiculous." It is not honest to treat them as ridiculous and negative, and at the same time claim the Christian heritage that flows directly from these claims. In this respect, I find the position of New Testament scholar Bart Ehrman,[14] who rejects his earlier Christian faith, to have far more integrity than the fuzziness of Bishop Spong,[15] who empties his Christian faith of most of the historical content the New Testament claims about the relationship between God and the human Jesus.

14. Ehrman, How Jesus.
15. Spong, New Christianity.

I very much agree with Bishop Spong's desire to mend the divide between Christians and Jews; however, his method of attempting to do so would cause me to reject following Jesus and being Christian altogether. I have no interest in following Jesus if his life, death, resurrection, and continuing life as God's first completed human in God's forever family are not something that God did in real human history. Whether the New Testament claims are true or not, neither Judaism nor Christianity can escape the fact that these New Testament claims originated as claims about God working with human in real space and time events.

The New Testament writers credit the origins of their before and after way of viewing what God has done through God's relationship with Jesus to Jesus himself. In Matthew 15:24–26 and 10:5–6, before his death and resurrection, Jesus says that being Jewish is definitely a privileged status, in terms of God's self-revelation through Jesus's current ministry. Then, in Matthew 28:16–20, after the crucifixion and resurrection, the resurrected Jesus tells his disciples that all nations are to be invited into a privileged relationship with God because of what God has done through Jesus.

Paul too sees Jesus as God's new historical act that moved history into a "new age" with a "new Adam" as God's "firstborn" of the "new creation." Paul's "dualism" is a before and after dualism that sees God changing history by exalting Jesus and by the outpouring of the Holy Spirit, which the Jewish prophet Joel had promised would inaugurate a new age.

This *before* and *after* was not a new way of understanding God's movement through human history because the Jewish narrative already saw history as a series of *befores* and *afters*. God's covenant with Abraham created a before and after, as did God's giving of the Torah through Moses. The Hebrew Bible sees Israelite history as before and after the Exodus liberation, Israel becoming a landed nation, God's covenant promises to King David, the division of the nation of Israel into North and South, and prior to exile in Babylon and after the exile. The wonderful Passover Seder prayer "Dayenu" ("It would have been enough") captures this ongoing paradigm of before and after experiences between God and humans.

Still, it is correct to say that the claims concerning Jesus were bound to cause an unresolvable tension between any Jewish person who did not think Jesus was the fulfillment of God's agenda for the Jewish people and anyone who thought he was, but it is not correct to say that the fulfillment theme was anti-Judaism or anti-Semitic. As Daniel Boyarin, who does not at all agree with their conclusions, maintains, these early followers of Jesus were stating a completely Jewish expression of an attempted resolution of first-century Jewish issues.[16]

THE FULFILLMENT THEME FLOWS FROM THE NEW TESTAMENT UNDERSTANDING OF HOW GOD'S PROMISES TO JEWS WERE ALWAYS INTENDED TO BLESS ALL OF HUMANITY.

The New Testament claims concerning Jesus's place in God's purpose for the entire world makes sense only if they are a development within the Old Testament context promising that God wanted to bless all nations of the world through Abraham's descendants. Whether or not you believe that God truly was fulfilling God's promises to Abraham through God's relationship with Jesus, it is important to see that the claims are rooted in this Hebrew Bible understanding of the "mission" of the Jewish people. Not only the original covenant promise to Abraham (Gen 12:1-3), but also many other Old Testament texts, claim that God wanted to bless the entire world through the descendants of Abraham. As Isaiah (or Second Isaiah and Third Isaiah, if you prefer) prophesied about God's purpose long ago:

> He [YHWH] says: "It is too small a thing for you to be my servant to restore the tribes of Jacob and bring back those of Israel I have kept. *I will also make you a light for the Gentiles, that you may bring my salvation to the ends of the earth.*" (Isa 49:6; emphasis mine)

16. Boyarin, Jewish Gospels, and Radical Jew.

Exodus 19:5–6 introduces the giving of the ten command-ments through Moses with the promise and challenge that YHWH is choosing Israel to be "priests" who will be God's mediators for all other people groups, so the idea that all nations were to be blessed by and through the descendants of Abraham and Sarah was cer-tainly not a new thought.

It is in this context that the New Testament provides a "be-fore and after" understanding of how God wants Israel to be God's agent in fulfilling this promise to bless all nations. This claim was (and is) bound to cause tension with every Jewish person who does not think God created a "before and after" in God's relationship with Jesus.

The big-picture story in the New Testament is the claim that God moved these promises toward overwhelming fulfillment through God's relationship with a first-century Jewish human named Jesus. The relationship between God and Jesus was such that God honored Jesus's complete faithfulness to God, a faithful-ness that involved being an observant Jewish keeper of Torah, a worshipper every Sabbath in the synagogue, a worshipper at the Temple in Jerusalem, and a teacher of Torah.

All of Jesus's faithful love for God and for his fellow humans is expressed within the context of the covenant with Abraham, the Torah given by Moses, the promises made to King David, and the soaring future hopes of the Prophets. Even Jesus's death is pictured by New Testament writers as the faithful fulfillment of the death of the Passover lamb on the table of the Jewish Seder. The New Tes-tament writers claim that, by following this execution with Jesus's resurrection and exaltation as Lord of the next age of human his-tory, God made a way to incorporate Gentiles into the Israel of God.

Again, there is no legitimate way to resolve the tension this New Testament master narrative creates between those who trust that God was and is keeping his ancient promises in this manner through Jesus and those who are certain that this is not true. How-ever, we can present the original intent far more accurately than it is often presented.

New Testament Writers Are Clear—Fulfillment Does Not Mean Replacement.

The early church fathers such as Tertullian, Augustine, and Chrysostom, in their increasingly Gentile church setting, taught that God had replaced and rejected the Jews. This contrasted with Paul, who, even though he runs a close second to the authors of the Gospels of John and Matthew in being problematic for modern Jewish people, did not see being Jewish as having become "irrelevant." He was a follower of Jesus, and he was still proud to self-identify as a Jew (Rom 3:1ff and 9:1ff and Gal 2:14–15). He continued to draw personal comfort when "coworkers of the circumcision" were around him as he ministered (Col 4:10–11). If, as some scholars think, an author much later than Paul wrote Colossians, it is an even stronger and later indication that followers of Jesus were continuing to hold tightly to their Jewish roots.

On the other hand, Paul does present God's new act through God's relationship with Jesus as having changed what it means for him to be Jewish. Both in Romans and Galatians, Paul argues that, just as before God's covenant with Abraham, there was no privileged ethnic or cultural status in God's process of self-revelation through human history, it is now again true that God's revelatory purpose in history includes no privileged ethnic or cultural status. Before Abraham, it was true because God had not yet moved forward in history with the step that ultimately created Israel. After Jesus, it is true because God has moved his promise to Abraham forward to its next step. Paul thinks it is still good to be proud of being Jewish and to be comforted by fellow cultural ethnicity, but God has acted in such a manner that being Jewish is no longer a privileged ethnic or cultural status in God's revelatory historical purpose.

Paul maintains that this claim of *no continuing privileged status* once fueled his violence toward followers of Jesus, but now it makes him excited to be a part of God's new forward movement in history. He credits the difference to experiencing that God did in fact raise Jesus from death and exalt him to the right hand of God. In effect, Paul claims to have experienced that Stephen was right and honest in his vision of Jesus, while Paul was at that point honest but wrong in his opposition to the threat he thought Stephen posed to God's previous self-revelation (Acts 7:54–8:3).

In both Paul's and Matthew's writings, fulfillment is understood in terms of God's historical process and thus as a "before and after" dynamic. The New Testament claim is that everything God did before Jesus was God's preparation for what God was going to do for all humanity through God's relationship with Jesus. The relationship shared by God and Jesus in Jesus's life, death, resurrection, ascension, and exaltation/reign has allowed God to move toward God's final goal for human history.

Jewish privilege in God's historical purpose is not being rejected by the claims to fulfillment, but it is seen as a stage in God's larger historical process, so after Jesus, the privileged status of sonship and daughterhood has been opened to people of all cultures. Being Jewish is still a delight for Paul, but no longer a privileged cultural status in God's forward progress toward making humans into the image and likeness of God as members of God's forever human family—the Kingdom of God.

Fulfillment as Continuity Rather than Rejection Is a Hebrew Bible Pattern.

Whether the New Testament claim of fulfillment without rejection was (and is) right or wrong, it was not an idea created by these writers. It was in continuity with a long-standing pattern in the Hebrew Bible. The writers of the Old Testament did not see the fulfillment of earlier patterns as a negation of how YHWH worked in earlier history. God choosing Abraham and Sarah is not presented as a replacement of God's concern for all nations, but as a step of fulfillment that involves God's concern for all nations (Gen 12:1–3).

Exodus 19:5–6 claims that God's decision to create Israel as a nation of "priests" for the world is not a replacement of God's concern for all nations, but rather a step of fulfillment in God's concern for all nations. The building of the First Temple is not a rejection of Israel's earlier worship centered in the Tabernacle ("Tent of Meeting"); rather, it fulfills the earlier pattern. Isaiah 40 is not demeaning or rejecting the "exodus" from Egypt when it prophesies a fulfillment of the pattern in a new exodus from Babylon and Persia. This re-creation of the nation of Israel is not a replacement, but rather a next step, and thus a fulfillment of the long history of God's relationship with Israel.

Most Jews of later times did not see the reuse of the Exodus theme by Isaiah 40 describing God's work with those who left Babylon for Israel as delegitimizing the ongoing Jewish community that chose to remain in Babylon. Even though the original Exodus would not have honored staying in Egypt, the reuse of the pattern for return did not delegitimize the center of Jewish Scriptural understanding and rabbinic training that grew up around those who chose to stay in Babylon. Fulfillment without supersession made sense, and patterns could be reused without replacement and rejection. Isaiah 19 speaks of God's future bringing about a day when Assyria, Egypt, and Israel will, through God's merciful activity, be able to worship YHWH together, yet the book of Isaiah does not see this "fulfilment" of God's promise to Abraham as delegitimizing Israel's current history as a "separate" people who need to trust YHWH to "save" them from the Empires of Assyria and Egypt (See Isa 7, 10, 14, and 30).

Fulfillment that is not rejection is a concept drawn directly from the Old Testament narratives and prophecies by Jesus and by the writers of the New Testament. The idea that fulfillment means "rejection" of the past was not inherent in the New Testament concept of fulfillment any more than it was in the Old Testament. Both Testaments often see God's actions that "fill full" earlier patterns with new acts of God as creating a "before" and "after," but not as creating "rejection" of the "before." In fact, as we will see in the next chapter, many times New Testament authors made it clear that they neither rejected the Judaism of others nor their own Jewish faith and ethnicity. Sadly, the same cannot be said about how the New Testament was reinterpreted in Christian history.

8

New Testament Authors Did Not Intend to Be Anti-Judaism or Anti-Semitic.

"FULFILLMENT" DID NOT CAUSE EARLY FOLLOWERS OF JESUS TO EXPECT THE END OF JUDAISM.

ANOTHER IMPORTANT REASON I do not think the New Testament writers saw fulfillment as replacement is that quite a few New Testament passages indicate an expectation that Jewishness, Israel, and synagogue worship would continue indefinitely. Living during a first-century argument over who rightfully understood God's next steps in Jewish history, the writers could not have foreseen how the power dynamics would change in the future, but there is no indication they saw the continuation of Judaism as negative.

In fact, though many Christians have held that the New Testament writers thought Jesus meant the end of Judaism, there is strong evidence to the contrary. Acts 15:5 identifies some of the followers of Jesus as "believers from the party of the Pharisees." Acts also presents Paul's team as being welcomed in some synagogues and forced out of synagogue worship in others. Paul responds angrily to some specific Jewish leaders, delights in others, but never implies that Jewish assemblies across the Roman world should cease to exist.

Commentators sometimes interpret Acts 15:21 as indicating that Moses's Torah has been preached and read in the past, but now something new is replacing it. Sadly, some English translations make this sound like a past event, although both Greek verbs are present tense, indicating an ongoing reality. It seems to me, given the Greek tenses and the quite conservative Jewish stance ascribed to James throughout the New Testament, the best way to hear the passage is as a statement that he expects God to sustain synagogue worship indefinitely, regardless of decisions concerning Jesus. In fact, James's words are still true today: "Moses has those who are preaching him in every synagogue and reading him every Sabbath."

According to Acts 21, followers of Jesus, including leaders like Paul and James, continued to worship in the Temple for many years. Though written by the Gentile Luke, the following quotation states clearly that Jews who follow Jesus are still "Jews" who still "follow the Law (Torah)." It also maintains that Paul never taught Jews to abandon the law of Moses, even though it was rumored that he had been doing so.

> [20]When they heard this, they praised God. Then they said to Paul: "You see, brother, how *many thousands of Jews have believed, and all of them are zealous for the law.* . . . [24]Take these men, join in their purification rites and pay their expenses, so that they can have their heads shaved. *Then everybody will know* there is no truth in these reports about you, but *that you yourself are living in obedience to the law.*" (Acts 21:20–24; emphasis mine)

Paul expects Jewish people to still be Jewish until the end of human history (Rom 11). The Gospel of Luke indicates that Jesus, too, expected Jewish people to still be worshipping God as Jews when "the times of the Gentiles will be fulfilled" at the "end of the present age" (Luke 21:24).

In Acts, Luke indicates that the followers of the risen Jesus still correctly anticipate a future time when God "restores the kingdom to Israel," even though it will not occur as soon as they are hoping it will. Instead, Jesus sends them out to be another incarnation of the Jewish Diaspora as they wait for the final "restoration of Israel" (Acts 1:5–8).

The casual use of the Greek root word for "synagogue" to describe "church" gatherings of Jesus's followers in James 2:2 and 2 Thessalonians 2:1 indicates that no rejection of "the synagogue" was contemplated. Sadly, Christian translators have tended to hide this connection. The fact that these same translators have no hesitancy to use "synagogue" when translating Revelation 2:9 (exactly the same Greek word as James 2:2), where it is used negatively of some Jewish leaders who are persecuting some followers of Jesus, tells us far more about modern Christian anti-Judaism than it does about the New Testament context.

Although I can easily point to New Testament passages that indicate an expectation similar to that of Jeremiah and Ezekiel, stating that specific Jewish people (usually leaders) were taking a stand against God's desires, I do not see anything that would indicate that any New Testament author expected God to abandon the synagogues or the Jewish people in general. On the other hand, there are many indications that the New Testament writers did not think Judaism would or should disappear. They seem to have left it for God to work out what this would mean for those who followed Jesus and those who did not.

"Fulfillment" is a central New Testament teaching. "Abandonment," "rejection," and "replacement" are not, except in the same ways these concepts appear in Isaiah, Ezekiel, Hosea, and Zechariah. New Testament talk of rejection is always focused on leaders who should know better than doing whatever they are doing, not on a rejection of Jews by God. Whether you think that the Old Testament prophets and the New Testament writers were right or wrong in their claims, the claims are much the same.

We desperately need to revisit the church's interpretation of Biblical materials and their description of the relationship between God and Jesus, which were almost all anti-Judaism (religion) and increasingly anti-Semitic (ethnic/racial/cultural) from the second through the nineteenth centuries. The need to revisit can easily be seen from the scholarly works of writers such as James D. G. Dunn, Amy-Jill Levine, Larry Hurtado, Daniel Boyarin, and Bart Ehrman. Some of these authors might agree on little else, but each concludes that the texts we call the New Testament are deeply rooted in first-century Jewish thinking and Jewish paradigms and were not announcing an end to Judaism.

NEW TESTAMENT WRITERS CONTINUED TO SELF-IDENTIFY AS JEWS.

However problematic it became for the early church fathers, and then later for Jewish people in response to the bitterness of the church fathers, the early followers of Jesus identified themselves far more often as "Jews" than they did as "Christians." This is yet another reason I think fulfillment was never meant by New Testament writers to be understood as an end to Judaism.

Every New Testament writer other than Luke continues to either explicitly or to implicitly self-identify as a Jew who is a follower of Jesus. Obviously, other first-century Jewish leaders thought they were wrongheaded in following Jesus as the Messiah. However, it is highly unlikely that anyone in the first century would have thought that they were claiming to have left their Jewish heritage and faith for a new religion. In fact, if they had appeared to be starting a new religion, instead of claiming to be the fulfillment of the prophetic promises, it would have been much easier for the Jewish leaders who disagreed with them to ignore them.

In the entire New Testament literature, only one writer ever identifies as "Christian" (1 Pet 4:16). The two other uses of the term "Christian" in the New Testament are ambiguous and may even be sarcastic uses of the term by people who were not followers of Jesus (Acts 11:26 and 26:28).

In contrast to the very rare identification as Christian in the New Testament, New Testament followers of Jesus are regularly identified as "Jews." The Gentile writer of Acts quotes both Stephen and Paul as referring to Jewish people who do not believe Jesus to be God's Messiah as "brothers" (see for examples Acts 7:2ff, 22:1, 23:1, and 28:17ff, as well as Acts 13:15, where the synagogue ruler greets Paul and Barnabas as "brothers").

In Romans 9:3, Paul uses the same Greek word "brothers" (*adelphoi*) to designate Jewish people who do not follow Jesus that he also uses throughout this same letter of Romans to designate both Jews and Gentiles who are following Jesus. As mentioned previously, in Galatians 2:14–15 Paul states clearly in front of a predominantly Gentile congregation that both he and Peter are still "Jews" in a religious sense. In Colossians 4:11, decades into his ministry, Paul claims great comfort in having a few coworkers who are "of the circumcision," a deeply emotional identification of these followers of Jesus—and of himself—as ethnically and culturally still Jewish. If you are among those who think Colossians was not written by Paul, the point still stands, perhaps even more strongly, that some still later writer thought it very important to continue identifying Paul and part of his team as "of the circumcision."

GOD RAISING JESUS FROM DEATH IS PRESENTED IN A JEWISH CONTEXT.

Obviously, I believe that the New Testament claim that God raised Jesus from death in order to begin a new stage in human history is true. However, whether it is true or not, it was a thoroughly Jewish claim. C. S. Lewis could well be right in claiming that in raising Jesus, God also fulfilled the hopes represented in many Gentile myths of "dying and rising gods"; however, these myths rarely bear any resemblance to the New Testament context. It is the Old Testament understanding that God is committed to humans and values the material creation that is the underlying foundation for the New Testament claim that God raised Jesus with a "glorious body" (Phil 3:21).

In the New Testament writings themselves, the resurrection of Jesus occurs totally within a Jewish context. In addition to the emphasis on bodily resurrection as a part of the renewal of creation, there are other ways the claims concerning God raising Jesus from death are grounded in Judaism. Reread the New Testament with this question in mind: "Who is the first Gentile whom the New Testament records as seeing the risen Jesus?" You will find that not even one Gentile ever sees the resurrected Jesus in any New Testament writing—a strange reality if the goal of the writers was to place Jesus within the framework of Gentile mythology.

Another way the resurrection of Jesus is embedded in the first-century Jewish context is that it reflects the growing Jewish understanding that there can be no hope for God's justice for individuals apart from God raising the dead. This is not to say that any Jewish person expected a final resurrection after three days to occur in the middle of history for one person. As far as we know, no one did. This includes the followers of Jesus, who are described as losing all hope and running for their lives when Jesus is executed.

However, a final resurrection hope as a culmination of this era of history seems to have become a central part of the understanding of the Pharisees, according to Josephus, Acts 23, and later Rabbinic literature. Apparently, the Dead Sea Qumran community also had some people who looked for resurrection of the dead, according to scroll 4Q521 from Cave 4. The book of 2 Maccabees, that most scholars date as written prior to the time of Jesus, clearly describes such a faith in a Jewish mother. Jon D. Levenson, writing from a modern scholarly Jewish perspective,[17] and N. T. Wright, from a modern scholarly Christian perspective,[18] provide extensive evidence that God raising humans from death as the beginning of a "new age" in human history was a hope shared by some, perhaps many, first-century Jews.

As far as we know, resurrection of humans was not a major expectation of any Gentile philosophy or religion. Some had intimations of "immortal souls" and "atmans" and "God-sparks" that might or might not survive death, but no Gentile philosophy or religion hoped for a permanent resurrection to a forever life in a forever family of God. Most Gentile religious and philosophical thought would have considered resurrection of the body to be

17. Levenson, Resurrection and Restoration.
18. Wright, Resurrection of Son.

counter to the need to escape the limitations of the physical body. But, for quite a few first-century Jews, the hope of resurrection was increasingly seen as the only way for God to fulfill God's love for humans as well as the only way God could bring justice for those who had suffered terribly while serving God. It might be that some had also begun to see future resurrection as the only way we humans could expect any final resolution to our current political dilemmas. How else can God be faithful to what Jews and Christians have believed God promises to do for individual humans?

I would make the same argument concerning God-seeking Jewish people who were slaughtered in the Holocaust. In my opinion, only a future resurrection could possibly offer any justice and any ultimate fulfillment of their faith or of their humanity, because they certainly received none from Nazis, or from the rest of the world, during their lifetime. In fact, isn't it true that there can be no justice for the millions of humans who for many millennia have lived lives of constant unjust suffering and hurt and died with no reparations, unless there is a future time for God to act to bring justice for them?

Personally, I think that if God is in any sense truly good and really loving, then resurrection of humans to be with God forever as God's forever family is the only resolution to the Biblical claims, written by mostly Jews, that God's relationship with us humans is a relationship of love and caring. I am not overly good, and I am less than sterling at loving, but I would do anything I could to be with the people I love—as their genuine human selves—forever. If God is real, cares about us humans, and loves us for the persons we are, surely God's caring must be better than mine. If God is faithful in wanting to relate to us humans, then this trustworthiness must result in something that God has not yet done for us or for those who have gone before us. If God loves you, God wants to be with you forever.

The trust I am expressing concerning God's faithfulness guaranteeing God's intention to raise humans from death, I owe to Jewish experiences with God recorded in Psalms, Prophets, and New Testament writings, brought to life again by the Spirit of God in my life. From Plato to Machiavelli to Darwin, no Gentile philosophy would lead me to this trust in God.

THE GOSPEL OF MATTHEW COULD JUST AS EASILY BE SEEN AS ANTI-GENTILE, AS ANTI-JEWISH.

To keep this section brief, I will focus primarily on the Gospel of Matthew. However, I think a similar approach can be taken for almost any New Testament writing, including the Gospel of John, which expresses a great deal of frustration with the political and religious hierarchy of the day, but not with Jewish faith, worship, or ethnicity. Both Matthew and John are texts that cause great problems today because they are laden with millennia of Christian misuse in ways that have been very anti-Semitic and anti-Judaism. Of course, this interpretive history must now be reckoned with. The texts are now laden with that history.

Having said that, it is also helpful to acknowledge that this horrible history did not exist when these books were written. They were written with the same intrafamily squabbling characteristics we see in some of the Dead Sea Scrolls and in the power struggle among various Jewish sects prior to the Roman destruction of the Temple in 70 AD.

Many scholars claim Matthew is a very anti-Judaic and perhaps even an anti-Semitic Gospel. Many Christians, both conservative and liberal, justify their continuing anti-Judaism from passages in Matthew. Some far-right conservatives go farther and justify anti-Semitism as well. This approach to Matthew is supposedly validated both by the antagonism Matthew describes between Jesus and some Pharisees, the antagonism the High Priestly clan is described as having toward Jesus, and by references such as Matthew 10:17—"Beware of them, for they will hand you over to the council (Sanhedrin) and flog you in their synagogues"—which has been read in churches for centuries as justification for anti-Semitism and anti-Judaism. It would have been much truer to the text's original purpose if it had been reapplied as a meaningful warning to the "Christians" who led the Catholic Inquisition, burned fellow Protestants at the stake, and lynched fellow American Christians because they were black.

Matthew's Gospel is very Jewish in its style and its concerns. Among these concerns is Matthew's presentation of Jesus's view of the brokenness of first-century Gentile cultures. In fact, without too much stretching, the following quotations from Matthew could be understood to present a Jewish Jesus who was very anti-Gentile. I do not think Jesus or the writer of Matthew was actually anti-Gentile, but I think these quotations indicate that similar statements were not anti-Jewish either. It is possible to critique the weaknesses of cultures without being "*anti.*" As a current example, I think it imperative that we Americans learn to critique the past and present weaknesses of our American culture. I want this because I care about America and want it to be better, not because I am "anti-American."

What are the implications of the following quotations from Matthew's Gospel all using forms of *ethnos* in Greek though variously translated?

> [9]Then you will be handed over to be persecuted and put to death, and *you will be hated by all nations [ethnon] because of me.* (Matt 24:9; emphasis mine)

> [15]If your brother sins against you, go and show him his fault, just between the two of you. If he listens to you, you have won your brother over. [16]But if he will not listen, take one or two others along, so that "every matter may be established by the testimony of two or three witnesses." [17]If he refuses to listen to them, tell it to the church; and if he refuses to listen even to the church, *treat him as you would a pagan [ethnikos] or a tax collector.* (Matt 18:15–17; emphasis mine)

> [24]He [Jesus] answered, "*I was sent only to the lost sheep of Israel.*" [25]The [Canaanite] woman came and knelt before him. "Lord, help me!" she said. [26]He replied, "*It is not right to take the children's bread and toss it to their dogs.*" (Matt 15:24–26; emphasis mine)

[47] And if you greet only your brothers, what are you doing more than others? *Do not even pagans [ethnikoi] do that?* (Matt 5:47; emphasis mine)

[7] And *when you pray, do not keep on babbling like pagans [ethnikoi]*, for they think they will be heard because of their many words. [8] Do not be like them, for your Father knows what you need before you ask him. (Matt 6:7–8; emphasis mine)

[31] So do not worry, saying, "What shall we eat?" or "What shall we drink?" or "What shall we wear?" [32] *For the pagans [Ethna] run after all these things,* and your heavenly Father knows that you need them. (Matt 6:31–32; emphasis mine)

[5] These twelve Jesus sent out with the following instructions: "*Do not go among the Gentiles [ethnon]* or enter any town of the Samaritans. [6] Go rather to the lost sheep of Israel." (Matt 10:5–6; emphasis mine)

[25] Jesus called them together and said, "You know that *the rulers of the Gentiles [ethnon] lord it over them,* and their high officials exercise authority over them. [26] *Not so with you.* Instead, whoever wants to become great among you must be your servant. . . ." (Matt 20:25–26; emphasis mine)

Isn't it interesting how often Gentile Christian translators into English have managed to make several of these strong negative statements about "Gentiles" less vivid? If they were all translated as "Gentile," we would see just how prevalent the first-century Jewish critique of Gentile cultures is in Matthew's Gospel.

Only three semipositive passages about Gentiles occur in Matthew's Gospel, and even these three speak of the urgent need of the "Gentiles/nations" to receive the grace and mercy of God, as revealed through the Jewish people (Matt 28:18–20, 12:18–21 [quoting Isaiah,] and 25:31ff).

I acknowledge that both Matthew and John use the term "Jews" in a manner that is almost impossible today not to hear as anti-Semitic and anti-Judaism. If you think that I am trying too hard, and they did mean it as we now hear it, then let's learn from their mistake and do better. However, I don't think they meant their critiques the way we have been conditioned to hear them today. I think they were criticizing a very specific inner circle with economic, political, and religious power. And I think they were doing so in a manner similar to how some of us critique many Christian leaders today. With a few exceptions, every person they refer in their writings is "Jewish" in the ethnic sense that we use the term today.

Why do so many Christians and Jews tend to read Matthew/Jesus as rejecting "the Jews," while not even considering that they are at least as vehemently rejecting "the Gentiles"? It is because we have both implicitly and explicitly separated Jesus (and the Gospel writer) from his humanity as a Jew. Deep in our religious psyche, most of us tend to view Jesus as "the first Christian" and the New Testament as beginning a new "Gentile religion" called "Christianity." This substitution of "fulfillment" with "replacement" and "rejection" does become anti-Judaism and anti-Semitic.

Perhaps the nearly contemporary community of the Dead Sea Scrolls would describe the followers of Jesus as "sons of Satan," just as they described other Jewish groups they thought were mistaken. However, in both cases, it would be because they thought they were wrongheaded in their Judaism, not because they were not Jewish.

DISAGREEMENT WITHIN THE FAMILY WAS NOT ANTI-SEMITISM OR ANTI-JUDAISM.

The New Testament texts' use of the word "brothers" often reflects the fact that the early followers of Jesus related to Jewish people who were not followers of Jesus as "family." (Yes, I do wish they had said, "brothers and sisters," but that too is an honest reflection of the times.) Acts, written several decades after the cross–resurrection event, indicates that Peter, Paul, Stephen, and James all continued to freely refer to the Jewish people who were not followers of Jesus as "brothers" (Acts 7:2, 13:26, 22:1, 23:1, and 28:17). It would also be difficult to find a more poignant and persistent identification with the Jewish people than Paul's in Romans 3:1–3, 9:2–3, and 11:17–26, as well as in Colossians 4:10–11. Can we who claim these writers are our mentors in how to follow Jesus faithfully include their embrace of their Jewish "brothers" and "sisters" in our actions?

Who is "us," and who is "them?" It is not just specific texts, but also the overall context that convinces me that no New Testament writer was either anti-Semitic or anti-Judaism. Sadly, these texts can hardly be heard any other way today, and it is not just the early church, but also recent Christian scholarship that has made it almost impossible to read the New Testament any other way.

I have been arguing, as have others, that although New Testament writings can sound anti-Semitic, it is because later Christians used them to justify anti-Semitic attitudes while ignoring their original context as family squabbles. Family squabbles are not pleasant, but family members can say things to each other that non–family members cannot say, without changing the meaning of the words.

What the New Testament writers say about some Jewish people of their day is very similar to what Hosea, Isaiah, Jeremiah, Habakkuk and Joel had to say about many Jewish ("Israelite") people of their day, and nothing the New Testament writers critique about religious practices in Jesus's time differs essentially from the prophetic critiques of religious practices of priests and prophets by Isaiah, Jeremiah, Elijah, Elisha, Ezekiel, or the authors of 1 Samuel and 1 and 2 Chronicles. Furthermore, when we compare more recently discovered literature from Jesus's time to New Testament writings, we find that the New Testament writers' way of criticizing fellow Jews is completely consistent with, often milder than, the way other Jewish groups criticized each other.

It is important to think about why we do not consider the great prophetic figures of the Old Testament to be anti-Semitic or anti-Judaism and why no one accuses the writer of the apocryphal book of Tobit of being anti-Semitic or anti-Judaism, even though fellow Jews are described as idolaters and lawbreakers. The book of Susanna, which accuses prominent Jewish "elders" of attempted rape and of blackmail, is not considered anti-Semitic or anti-Judaism. Neither does it ever occur to us to claim that the writers of the Dead Sea Scrolls were anti-Semitic, even though the *War Scroll* identifies fellow Jews as "the sons of darkness," and as "the army of

Belial (demon-god)," while claiming that God will destroy them all. We know these were intra-family disputes.

The New Testament sounds anti-Semitic to us, whereas Hosea, Isaiah, Jeremiah, Ezekiel, Hosea, Tobit, Susanna, and the *War Scroll* do not sound anti-Semitic, not because New Testament writers are harsher or more critical in what they saw as a prophetic stance, but because many of us have been taught to identify Hosea, Isaiah, the writer of Susanna, and the authors of the Qumran Scroll as "one of them," and to identify New Testament writers, and implicitly Jesus himself, as "not one of them." We read the Dead Sea Scrolls, which were written during the same era, as reflecting an intra-family feud, though we have been taught to think of the "Christian" scriptures as a critique of Jews from the perspective of another religion: a tragedy that, as Amy-Jill Levine maintains, continues to be promulgated today by conservative and liberal Christians alike, though for differing reasons.

As I noted previously, instead of seeing the critiques of various leaders and various crowds as even more applicable to Christians than to anyone in Jesus's time, Christians have used words from the New Testament about some of the Jewish people of Jesus's time as weapons of mass destruction toward Jews. The following are only a few of many possible examples of how these family arguments became anti-Semitic platitudes.

Portrayal of Jewish Leaders

In movie after movie, book after book, and New Testament commentary after commentary, Jewish political and religious leaders in Jesus's time, and the various crowds that sometimes support them, are portrayed as people who walk on stage as obviously evil, while attempting to look holy. Did some of the High Priestly clan attempt to cover up greedy and oppressive actions with holy looks? Probably. But think of how many Christians, while proclaiming their own holiness, have compromised themselves with the horrors enacted at times by the Roman Empire, by the Inquisitions, by the disgusting

Papal compromises with Medieval Empires, and with the ethnic cleansing of Nazism.

The Crowds

Did some Jewish people in a crowd—no reason to think it was the same "crowd" that cheered him a week earlier, despite the beloved sermon material—jeer Jesus as he was led out to execution? Why would we doubt that, given that we see again and again how easily crowds are assembled and misled? Remember how crowds of most Christians gathered throughout the Jim Crow era of American politics to cheer lynchings that were scheduled as Sunday picnics— almost as "holy communion" gatherings—right after church services. Not to mention the jeering crowds made up of many calling themselves "Christian" that we see daily on our TV'S as they call for more bombing in the Middle East, speak of political opponents as "deplorables," and defend Judge Roy Moore's relationship with underage girls as modeling Joseph and Mary in the Bible.

The Pharisees

We Christians have in fact inexcusably turned the word "Pharisee" into an epithet for "arrogant, self-righteous" frauds. Perhaps the current tendency in the American press to use the word "Christian" to apply mainly to the religious far right is a proper judgment of God on all of us. It is certainly a good example to remind us of what we have done concerning "the Pharisees" and "the Jews." What we have done rivals what the media is currently doing. Did some Pharisees, and do some Christians, hold the views described when these labels are used? Yes. Is the label appropriate given the many Pharisees and the many Christians who actively live out other views and values? No.

I now cringe almost every time I hear the word "Christian" mentioned in the news—a vivid reminder of how Jewish people feel when they hear certain New Testament passages about "the Jews" read without context and without "some" as modifier. For example,

I heard several reports claiming that "Christians" or "the Christian Right" were the main support for Judge Roy Moore, with no acknowledgement that a large majority of those blacks, whites, and Hispanics who voted against him identify themselves as serious Christians who were voting their Christian values.

New Testament writers explicitly and implicitly say many positive things about the Pharisees. They are the group that have a theology closest to that of Jesus, as well as that of Paul, James, Peter, and Matthew. Pharisees are often Jesus's hosts for meals and are acknowledged in Acts as a sizable and influential group among the followers of Jesus (Acts 15). And, perhaps we Christians should note that no Pharisee is ever accused in the New Testament of abusing innocent children in the name of God, as many priests and pastors have been through the centuries and today.

Let's quit excusing what we Christians have done in turning the word "Pharisee" into an anti-Semitic and anti-Judaic epithet. What was written in the New Testament would have been heard then in the same way the constant critiquing of priests, pastors, popes, and Christians in general is heard today through Jim Wallis of Sojourners or in past generations through Dietrich Bonhoeffer and Fyodor Dostoevsky. The critiques are appropriately scathing in the mouths of these Christian critics, but they are in-house. The use of "pharisaical" by Christians has been far from in-house, and it is wrong. Have I committed this sin against Jewish people in past writings and sermons? Yes. Am I repentant? Yes! It is horribly wrong.

The Curse

"It is only by Beelzebub . . . this fellow drives out demons" is a comment recorded in the Gospels as the assessment of Jesus's healing power by some Jewish religious leaders (Matt 12:24). To my knowledge, no Christian preacher has ever preached a sermon saying that these words somehow became "God's words." Why then did "Let his blood be on us and on our children" from Matthew 27:25 come to be seen as a prophetic excuse for anti-Semitism and anti-Judaism by many Christians for many centuries? Obviously, consistency is not a priority when we desire to fuel our prejudices.

Do I wish that this statement were not in our New Testament? Yes, because it is now impossible to untangle it from centuries of abuse. It seems clear to me that Matthew saw the quotation much as I see the quotations from our current President's daily public Twitter account—the arrogant foolishness of leadership gone awry. (Please, do not discount the previous sentence as the words of a partisan Democrat. I am not a political Democrat, and I have plenty of critiques for them as well. I tend to vote as an Independent while holding my nose and wiping my tears.) When leaders make comments like this one quoted in Matthew now, or in the past, they are horrifying. They are not God's words, whether reported in Matthew or on the 6:00 p.m. news. They are arrogant words of compromised leaders, attempting to sound bold and confident concerning actions that are blatantly unjust, oppressive toward the disempowered, and politically motivated in the worst sense of the term.

How tragic that a sentence Matthew presents contextually, much as I might quote one of today's tweets from our current President, has for centuries been used as though it were a curse from God. It is probably impossible to undo this after all the generations of misuse. For that, we Christians need to be deeply repentant, and we need to quit reading the passage publicly, except when we take the time to clearly, completely, and competently reject the sinful way it has been used.

Judas/Jude/Jews

In Jesus's time the name "Judah/Judas" was a very honorable name reflecting the "fourth born" tribal ancestor, who ultimately inherited most of the role of "firstborn" among Jacob's many sons. It is used of at least eight different individuals in the New Testament—the tribal ancestor in the genealogies of both Matthew (Matt 1) and Luke (Luke 3:33), as an ancestor in the middle of Luke's genealogy (Luke 3:30), a brother of Jesus (Mark 6:3 and Jude 1), two of the men in Jesus's inner circle of disciples, one of whom becomes the betrayer (Luke 6:16 and Acts 1:13–16), a leader of a rebellion against Rome (Acts 5:37), the hospitable owner of the house where the blinded Paul sits waiting (Acts 9:11), and one of the Jewish leaders in the early Jesus's Movement as it expanded farther into Gentile territories (Acts 15:22–32). The name of the original tribal leader was also reflected in the name that came to describe the "Jewish" people (*Yehudaye* in Hebrew and *Ioudaioi* in Greek).

Sadly, many Christians have associated this honorable name primarily with the one "bad apple" among Jesus's apostles and turned this name with such a grand heritage into a dirty epithet. There is no escaping this history today. We must address it; however, I am suggesting that it does not reflect the New Testament literature. The New Testament used the name to designate many honorable individuals before and after the one traitor "Judas" and continued to use the tribal name of "Judah" to designate themselves as part of the community of "*Ioudaios*/Judeans/Jews." There is even a New Testament letter called "Jude."

The Problem Continues Today.

I acknowledge again that very understandably for many modern Jewish people where the horrible use of these New Testament passages began is far less important than the nineteen centuries of pain and destruction Christians have visited upon Jewish people. Perhaps it can help a little to entertain that the malicious anti-Semitism was imported into the original texts rather than flowing from their intent. However, it will not help much until we quit misusing these texts in the modern world.

The following are two of many possible examples illustrating how this ongoing tragedy continues. First, in a recent rereading of John's Gospel, I noticed that the section captions in my Bible included several captions such as "continuing unbelief of the Jews." These section headings are modern editorial additions to "help" the reader follow the train of thought. Usually, I just skip these additions, because I find them more bothersome than helpful, but this time I began to pay attention.

I found that beginning in chapter 1, and continuing through-out the Gospel, John several times speaks of "the Jews who believed in Jesus," of the Jewish crowds who praise Jesus, and of the Jewish leaders who follow Jesus, yet there was not a single caption reflect-ing "continuing belief of the Jews." Neither was there any caption or note that pointed out that Jesus and all of Jesus's followers were also "Jewish" as we use the term today. Christians are still being programmed ("helped?") by our Biblical editors to be anti-Semitic. The four Gospels record events claiming that thousands of Jewish people responded positively to Jesus as an authoritative prophet, teacher, and healer sent from God; yet there is no section heading that indicates this reality. Why no headings celebrating the "Jewish" synagogue leader who bows before Jesus in Matthew 9, Mark 5, and Luke 8?

Second, when Isaiah (6:9–12) says that, due to their hard-heartedness, his Jewish listeners cannot see, hear, or understand what God is attempting to say to them and to show them, it is not heard as anti-Semitic or anti-Judaism. However, when Jesus applies Isaiah's blast to his Jewish listeners, it is heard as anti-Judaism and often used to validate anti-Semitism (Mark 4:12). Many Christian commentaries exacerbate this problem by making anti-Judaic com-ments or by failing to point out that neither Isaiah nor Jesus was anti-Judaism. Of course, these same commentaries do not see it as anti-Christian when a few chapters later Jesus applies the same critique to his closest friends who also cannot "see" or "hear" the obvious (Mark 8:18–21). Consequently, week by week this passage is preached across the world by Christians as Jesus condemning "the Jews!"

I am not denying that frustration existed between the first-century Jewish people who saw the Jesus Movement as an evil or as a danger to both faith and culture, and the Jewish people who believed it was the work of God. That frustration is clear in many passages. Here, for example, is a text that hurts the ears when it is read today.

> [14]For you, brothers, *became imitators of God's churches in Judea [Ioudaia],* which are in Christ [Messiah]: You

> suffered from your own countrymen the same things those *churches suffered from the Jews [Ioudaion],* [15]*who killed the Lord Jesus and the prophets* and also drove us out. *They displease God* and are hostile to all men [16]in their effort to keep us from speaking to the Gentiles so that they may be saved. In this way they always *heap up their sins to the limit. The wrath of God has come upon them* at last. (1 Thess 2:14–16; emphasis mine)

I cannot imagine a Jewish person reading this passage today without cringing. I hope many Christians cringe as well, and I wish that we all did. Our hearing is filled with content from 1,800 years of abusive Christian interpretation and application. There is no way to undo that pain, but we who follow Jesus can begin saying more loudly that we are terribly sorry.

Only if we first lament our history is it appropriate to also attempt to hear this passage as originally an intrafamily argument, filled with intrafamily emotion, voiced by the part of the family that was feeling unjustly oppressed. The positive words in 1 Thessalonians 2:14a and the negative words in 2:14b–16b are all about "Jews." In fact, in Greek there was only minor difference in hearing *Ioudaia* (2:14) and *Ioudaion* (2:14b) read out loud, and they would have definitely been heard in the first century as referring to people of the same ethnicity. The writer of 1 Thessalonians was Jewish, so was his team of fellow ministers, and so were some of the original hearers in the fellowship at Thessalonica. Perhaps with some prayer and effort, we can at least begin to hear passages such as this more as we hear Jeremiah and Ezekiel's tirades against their Jewish peers, and less as they have sounded in the mouths of non-Jewish Christians for centuries. Can we?

If all of us today could hear these texts as Jews speaking to Jews, we would be hearing them correctly. Would this solve the differences between how Jews and Christians hear these words? Of course not! However, it would help us Christians confront some of the current misuse of these texts as though they were a "God-given" excuse for anti-Semitism and anti-Judaism.

And if modern Christians could see that the only correct way to interpret and apply these texts today is to critique ourselves and others as Christians, then we would be hearing the original messages correctly, and we would be treating our Scriptures as God's Living Word. To paraphrase Paul, surely it is clear today that "not all Jesus's people by name are truly Jesus's spiritual children," just as it was clear to the prophets that not all of Abraham's physical children were Abraham's spiritual descendants. I am no more anti-Christian in making that statement than Paul was anti-Semitic when he made his statements in Romans 3:1–3 and 9:1–7, or than Ezekiel was when he said Israel's unfaithfulness in his time was so bad that if they had still been alive, even the great and righteous intercessors Job, Noah, and Daniel could save only themselves.

I reemphasize: It is important that we learn, going forward, to read our New Testament with what should be, but often is not, an obvious reality in mind: Jesus, all of Jesus's apostles, all of Jesus's first followers, and all of the New Testament writers, except probably Luke, were Jewish, both by ethnicity and by faith. Many, perhaps most, of the earliest readers were Jewish as well. None of these writers and readers saw themselves as beginning a new religion. All of them understood what God had done in Jesus to be the next step toward the fulfillment of God's great purpose for humanity, proceeding from God's covenant with Abraham and Sarah, the history of Israel, and the writings of the Jewish prophets. Every one of them continued to see the Hebrew Bible as the proper source of revelation of the One God, not only to Israel, but to the world.

9

Followers of Jesus Have Been Big Losers Too.

JEWISH PEOPLE THROUGH THE centuries have suffered greatly due to the dual sins of Christian anti-Semitism and anti-Judaism. I have no intention of making this book about "our hurt," as though the victimizers can rightfully claim to be the primary victims. It is about our need for truth, tears, turning, and trusting. Far too often what we pretend is meant to address injustice ends up once again glorifying those privileged by both law and society. This can be seen in many current discussions of affirmative action, racial justice, gender equity, health care, and the rather meager "benefits" that have come to be labelled as "entitlements" by many of those who are far more *entitled* socially and legally. I once heard a New York lawyer who did not know he was being filmed respond to being questioned about whether or not he could further privilege a wealthy client at the expense of other people by saying, "Of course we can; who do you think actually writes these laws?" It is people with values like that who felt *entitled* to victimize people who paid social security tax all of their lives by calling what they paid for and are owed an *entitlement*. Writing as an entitled Christian in what is often labelled a "Christian nation" by some of my fellow Christians,

I need to watch myself carefully as I write about Jewish-Christian relationships.

Having acknowledged that as a Christian I am always in danger of twisting things so that everything focuses on us and our privilege, it is still important to focus on us—in the right way. It is always true that those who oppress others wound not only others, but also themselves, in the process. It is not just Jewish people who have been wounded by Christian anti-Semitism. Our anti-Semitism and anti-Judaism have affected church history in many tragic ways. We Christians have been, and continue to be, a wounded people because of our sins against the Jewish people. Abusers are always wounded through abusing others. Some of the ways it has been most costly to the church include the following:

1. Early in church history, it cost us a clear understanding of our Jewish roots and how they were meant to be the foundation for, and to sustain, the history of the Jesus Movement.
2. It has cost us a clear sense of the continuity and discontinuity with the Old Testament and its patterns of God's actions in human history that are essential to understanding the New Testament claims concerning the personal covenant relationship between God and Jesus.
3. It has also led to a lack of understanding that the many gifts that the New Testament writers claim God has given the church through Jesus's covenant relationship with God were a continuation of the Old Testament patterns of God's interactions with Israel.
4. It has led to terrible misunderstandings of the New Testament writers' attitudes and morality regarding "the Jews."
5. It has led to our misunderstanding of how New Testament writers understood the relationship between God and Jesus as a fulfillment and extension, not a replacement, of Israel's mission.
6. It has created a situation in which, after almost 2,000 years of anti-Semitism in the church's attitudes and interpretations of Scriptures, there is almost no good way to talk about the way

the Jewish New Testament writers viewed "fulfillment" that does not invite further anti-Semitic views in the present.

7. It has caused the loss of understanding of how deeply our Eucharist was embedded in the Passover Seder, which undoubtedly was practiced differently in the first century from the way it is today—but was still a celebration of liberation, community, and calling.

8. It has cost us a mutually supportive relationship with the faith community that, more than any other, shares our understanding of the "One God."

9. It has wounded us spiritually and psychologically, as oppressing others always does.

10. It has cost the average Christian many of the insights into the Hebrew Bible that are available through Jewish scholars. It has also often led to Christian scholars using these insights without crediting their source.

11. It has been a terrible witness to a watching world. Followers of a Jewish Jesus whom we call "the Prince of Peace" have for millennia displayed brutal hatred and violence toward Jesus's people.

12. It has helped facilitate our dehumanizing of the Jewish Jesus.

13. As the next chapter explores, it has led us to be debtors who refuse to acknowledge our indebtedness.

In victimizing and oppressing others, we have suffered many self-inflicted wounds.

10

Debts Followers of Jesus Owe the Jews

WHO LIKE TO BE told they are so far in debt that they can never repay the mounting obligations? Throughout this book, I have been claiming that the many sins of individual Christians and of the corporate church against Jewish people have left us—and are leaving us—in exactly that predicament. This chapter focuses not on our sins, but on the indebtedness we followers of Jesus should feel for the good gifts received from Jewish people and from Judaism. Still, I expect some Christians will not find the claims in this chapter to be endearing. That makes me sad, but not reticent. To all of us I say, "Let's grow up and face reality." The best way out of pain and problems is straight through. We all need to be shaken out of the privilege we have taken for ourselves and the arrogance it has fostered.

On the other hand, I am aware that the content of this chapter is unlikely to endear me to the many faithful Jewish people whom I consider brothers and sisters in our search for God. I wish it could, but such is the deep rift history has given us. That concerns me deeply. Perhaps at best, the content can be both somewhat frustrating and somewhat endearing. Having said that, we can move toward more trust only when we begin with truth, and what follows is my attempt to be truthful about some of what those of us who follow Jesus owe to the Jewish people, past and present. We probably owe a lot more, but certainly nothing less.

WE OWE TRUTH, TEARS, TURNING AND TRUSTING—AND MUCH MORE.

To reiterate a constant theme of this book. We who wish to follow Jesus owe our Jewish sisters and brothers the pattern of response that the biblical writers demand as the proper way to respond to our sins and failures: truth (confession), tears (repentance), turning (repentance), and trusting (believing that God will honor all the above).

In addition to owing our Jewish sisters and brothers our truth, tears, turning, and trustworthiness, we who wish to follow Jesus are also indebted to the Jewish people for much of the content of our faith and faithfulness. The following sections summarize some of what those of us who follow Jesus owe the Jews. Nothing about Jesus makes any sense outside of his original Jewish context. Nevertheless, most Christians have come to identify Jesus and the New Testament as "Christian," with little to no awareness that, long before they were "Christian," they were "Jewish."

As I noted earlier, the word *Christian* did not become popular until long after the New Testament was written. The New Testament was not written as an attempt to separate Christians from their Jewish roots. Instead, it is filled with acknowledgements of the indebtedness to the Jews owed by those who follow Jesus.

WE OWE THE JEWS FOR THE REVEALED EXPERIENCES THAT SHOW GOD IS "ONE," DEEPLY INVOLVED, GOOD, AND CARING.

The revelation of the "One God" who is not abstract, not many, not self-centered, and not capricious, but who is instead good, relational, purposeful, responsive, and personal, is a gift from God, preserved for us by the experiences and the writings of Jewish people. Many American Christians take this gift for granted, but it is never to be taken for granted. It is a startling revelation—"YHWH is our God, YHWH is One."

A few ancient religions and philosophies thought there was One God, but this "One" God tended to be a very abstract God. Others thought there was a High God above all other gods, who was mostly uninvolved in human history, while lesser gods filled that role in various ways. Some believed there was a high god over other gods who was at times involved with humans, but who would never be described as good, relational, purposeful, responsive, and personal toward humans. Still others taught that the many gods who interacted with humans were self-serving, rarely very good, and usually capricious.

I am not claiming that no one in the ancient world sought, worshiped, and served the One God as best they could; the Biblical writers certainly acknowledge these seekers. In the Old Testament we are introduced to incredible people such as Melchizedek, Job and his friends, Rahab, the Kenites, Ruth, Jethro the priest of Midian and Moses' father-in-law, and the newly enlightened Naaman. In the New Testament, we see a Canaanite mother whose love for her daughter is so compelling that it causes Jesus to change his mind and cross his own "good" ministry boundaries. In fact, she is the only person recorded to have won a theological argument with Jesus in any of the Gospel narratives (Matt 15:21–28). We also meet three Roman Centurions who are present in Roman Palestine as officers in a brutal occupying army, who, nevertheless, understand God and Jesus better than many of Jesus's closest friends (Matt 8:5–13; 27:54). Cornelius needs to be spoken to by the voice of heaven only once, and he obeys with joy. Peter needs to be spoken to by the voice of heaven three times, and he finally obeys with great reticence (Acts 10).

I am claiming that the impact of God's self-revelation as the One God, who is good, personal, responsive, and purposeful, came down through the ages to us through the Jewish people, not through Gentile God-seekers. For this we owe the Jews.

WE OWE THE JEWISH PEOPLE FOR EXPERIENCING HISTORY AS PURPOSEFUL.

We owe the Jewish people for living and preserving a history of God's self-revelation, unlike any other in the world in terms of purposefulness. This debt is related to the revelation of the One God, but it is so central that it needs to be celebrated for its own uniqueness. We owe God and the Jewish people for the understanding that God is working toward a goal in human history. History is not circular. History is not meaninglessness attempting to lift itself by our own human bootstraps.

This understanding of history has so deeply influenced the world that, as the Jewish–Christian understanding of purposeful history spread around the world, even people who did not believe in God often adopted a purposeful view of history. Darwinism came to be presented by many as *inevitable progress* in natural selection, and Social Darwinism and even Atheistic Communism claimed human history is a process of *inevitable progress*. These movements are appropriately being questioned today, given that any claim of inevitable progress is empirically unjustifiable. My point here is that they reflected the impact of Jewish-Christian historical purpose and then imported the "inevitable" in the place of God's love and purpose for humans.

For a follower of Jesus, history is the playing out of God's purpose for creating the universe and for creating humans. It is about relationships. Human history has a purpose and a goal because the One God has a purpose and a goal. God is creating a forever family. The history of Creation, Covenant with Abraham and Sarah, Exodus, Torah, Covenant through David, Prophets, Exile, and Return are all events that tell us more of what God is like than we could ever know otherwise—and they give more meaning to our human history than we could ever have imagined.

Every time we followers of Jesus move away from the purposeful and personal worldview given to us through the experiences of God recorded for us in the Old Testament, we quickly revert to pagan ways of religion and culture. This reversion takes different forms for different personalities. For me personally, it involves a regression into the paganism that emphasizes and experiences meaninglessness and boredom—*ennui.*

For others, it means reverting to being dominated by the fearfulness that haunts much of the world and makes us humans so vulnerable to dictators and charlatans, as well as to evil spirits— whether personal demons or cultural demons, such as Nazism. For others, it means reentering the powerful spiritual realities created by the greedy lust for power, money, and sexual conquest at all cost. For still others, it means once again giving in to the depression, or to the self-indulgence, that haunt other parts of the pagan world. For others still, it means turning back to the worship of the Empire, its flag, and its newest leader, as pagan cultures have done for thousands of years. If we are not to be fully conformed to the various pagan forces of this world, it will be because we are embracing the transforming purposefulness of God in human history. A debt we owe the Jews.

WE OWE THE JEWS FOR JESUS.

We owe the Jewish people for giving us Jesus—genetically, historically, and in every other way. According to New Testament writers, the Messiah and Savior from God could not have been born in any culture other than Jewish culture because he flows from promises made to people such as Abraham, Sarah, Moses, David, and Isaiah. The writer of Hebrews 6:13–20 believed that the Messiah had to be Jewish, or God would have proven to be a liar. Paul makes much the same point in Romans 9–11.

Jesus is described in the Gospels as Jewish through and through. He is introduced as the "son of David" who will fulfill the promises God made to David (Luke 1:27 and 1:32–33). He customarily worships in synagogue on the Sabbath, as well as at the Temple in Jerusalem during the high holy days. He knows the Hebrew Bible and applies it in traditional Jewish ways. He wears the "fringes" on his garments that the Torah commanded (Luke 8:44—the almost certain meaning of the word often translated "hem" or "edge"). He observes the Passover regularly. He is executed with the sign "King of the Jews" hanging over his head. His resurrection and his appearances after the resurrection are all observed only by people who are Jewish. In short, Jesus was a very Jewish person, born into a long history that formed his teachings, his actions, and his relationship with God. He is never described as "the first Christian"; he is consistently described as a faithful and observant Jew.

Jesus's faith, teachings, and actions flowed directly out of his trust that the God who was revealed in the experiences recorded in the Old Testament narratives was the God he was experiencing as *Abba*. Jesus never rejected the earlier experiences of God as they were recorded in the Old Testament: he always claimed to be revealing more of who that God is, not a different God. Jesus responded to those Scriptural texts as God-given guides for his life and growth as a faithful human.

Yes, there is a new way of telling the Old Testament story in the light of what God is revealing about God's-self through God's relationship with Jesus, but this fulfills; it does not replace either the Hebrew Bible or the God who revealed God's-self in the experiences recorded there. Not for Jesus; not for Jesus's early followers. The retelling of God's history with humans, focused on God's relationship with Jesus, is truthful and genuine only if it is based fully in the first telling of the story God had been writing for millennia prior to Jesus, as it is told in the ancient narratives of the Old Testament.

My wife and I shared an experience that helped illustrate for us these two ways to tell the same story. Not too long ago, my wife endured 18 months of increasing pain in her leg, hip, knee, and back. Professionals took two MRIs and several x-rays. A Harvard-educated surgeon told her she did not need a hip replacement, while insulting her by refusing to listen to her experiences and by suggesting she was exaggerating her pain in order to have surgery— he certainly did not know my wife! A doctor skilled at injecting cortisone into "just the right spot" tried to help, but nothing positive occurred. A very skilled physical rehab doctor kindly spent far more time and effort than we expected, attempting to ascertain the cause of all the pain and was honest in saying, "I just don't know what is causing all your pain." An amazingly skilled deep message therapist relieved the pain for a short time on several occasions, but the relief didn't last beyond a few hours. Many friends, some in medical fields, made other suggestions, but eventually, everyone shrugged their shoulders and said, "It is a mystery; I cannot figure it out." That is one true and accurate way of telling our story.

Then our family physician told my wife, "I think you should get a second opinion from a different surgeon." This surgeon looked over all the past notes, had my wife turn in a different direction while keeping her weight fully on the painful leg, and took a new x-ray. A few minutes later, he walked into the room, flashed the picture up on the screen, and said, "Mystery revealed, and I can fix it! A hip replacement is the only thing that will help." And thank God, it did! A few months later, she was walking the trails in the Rocky Mountains.

We now have a second story to tell, but it is completely embedded in and flows from the first story. The "before" story is a story of historical process involving one event after another, all moving us forward and providing important information, but none of which shone a clear light on the bigger picture. Often, the story seemed to be going nowhere fast, and at other times it was just very confusing. Much like people attempting to figure out the prophecies of old concerning God's coming salvation, things had been revealed in bits and pieces, but no one could fit them into a clear, big picture because a key part was yet to be revealed.

Our second story is the story of *after* that *aha moment,* when something no one could figure out was suddenly revealed from an entirely different perspective. Suddenly the unclear was clarified because the key had been uncovered. Obviously, this successful surgeon is not God. Nevertheless, his moment of revelation was an amazing moment for us, as we experienced the uncovering of what had previously been a mystery, but now suddenly became a *now you can see it* moment of revelation. Our new way of telling the story makes sense only if it flows directly from how we first experienced the story.

At least for us, this experience helps a bit in understanding the *aha moments* the followers of Jesus experienced when the risen Jesus appeared to them. Then the continuing *aha moments* such as the one Peter and his friends experienced a few years later, when they saw a Gentile Roman army officer, Cornelius, receive an out-pouring of God's Spirit right in front of their eyes (Acts 10–11). These events were fully embedded in the covenant with Abraham and Sarah that was to bless all nations for all time—but who could have guessed? No one! Nevertheless, the story makes sense only as embedded in its original foundations.

WE OWE THE JEWS FOR THE CONTENT OF THE ROLES ASSIGNED TO JESUS.

Jesus makes sense only within the Jewish context. This includes all of Jesus's roles and titles, as well as the functions he exercises in his relationship with God. Jesus as Prophet, High Priest, King, Messiah, Savior, Suffering Servant, and Lord are fully informed by Jesus as Jewish. Many of these roles existed in other cultures, but it was Jewish history with God that gave them the content that Jesus fills with new depth. Jesus is fully embedded in the Old Testament history that gave these titles their New Testament content.

For example, ignoring the meaning of the role of Jesus as Jewish Prophet has reenforced some of the horrible anti-Semitism and anti-Judaism of church history. Jesus did criticize some of the Jewish Temple leaders, some of the Pharisees who were popular teachers, and some of the attitudes of some of the everyday Jewish people, just as Isaiah did, just as Ezekiel did, just as Hosea did, and just as Jeremiah did. The role of the Jewish prophet was to call the Jewish people back to the relationship with God and with their fellow humans that God wanted for them.

Failure to see Jesus as in the line of these Jewish Prophets has led to loading his words with anti-Semitic and anti-Judaic content. It never occurs to us to make that claim about the words of the Prophets of old because we identify them as Jewish Prophets. That is one of the key ways the New Testament identifies Jesus as well. But it has not been the way Christians have tended to identify Jesus. We have tended to identify him as the first anti-Jewish "Christian" prophet. How sad!

The fiery critiques in the *War Scroll* from Qumran that describe fellow Jews as "the sons of darkness" and as "the army of Belial (demon-god)" are identified as in-house prophetic critiques. We would never think of them as anti-Semitic, even though they make the words attributed to Jesus's prophetic ministry seem tame.

Many of the words of Hosea, Isaiah, Jeremiah, Ezekiel, and John the Baptizer also make Jesus's words sound pretty tame. Jesus's words (and those of his followers) are no more anti-Jewish than the searing critiques of many Christians by Christian writers like Bonhoeffer, Dostoevsky, Kierkegaard, and Martin Luther King Jr. were anti-Christian. Pope Francis vehemently criticizes Christians almost daily. Who would accuse Pope Francis of being anti-Christian?

WE OWE THE JEWS FOR OUR BIBLE.

We owe Jewish people for the book we call "the Bible" or "Our Scriptures." Over 90% of the Old Testament comes to us written by Jewish people. Job, several sections of Proverbs, and perhaps a paragraph here and there are the only exceptions. Even less emphasized by many Christians, the entire New Testament is also written by Jewish people, with the likely exception of the two books written by Luke. Even the Gospel of Luke and the book of Acts, though apparently written by a Gentile, spend over 90% of their content speaking about Jewish people and Jewish issues.

Beyond the writers, the price in time, resources, and sometimes even lives, that Jewish people paid through the centuries to save the Hebrew Bible for us has been very high. We who are Gentile followers of Jesus would not have anything close to the reliable texts that we do have, if Jewish people had not been willing to pay these costs.

WE OWE THE JEWS FOR THE LANGUAGE AND FOR THE PATTERNS THROUGH WHICH GOD SPEAKS TO US TODAY.

Exploration of various words and patterns from both the Old Testament and the New Testament fills many Christian books. We are not, however, always careful to identify these words and patterns as gifts from God, given to us and preserved for us through the Jewish people.

Words

A few of many possible examples of language filled with content by the narratives written by Jewish authors of both the Old and New Testament follow. I am not claiming that no other religion prior to Jesus had related concepts; I am claiming that the experiences recorded in the Old Testament and the New Testament are laden with a way of understanding these categories that is a unique revelation from God.

Forgiveness as "grace," rather than as a tit-for-tat business transaction. This gracious forgiveness is an essential means to the goal of real, deepening relationships. This forgiving is the lifting of burdens we could never carry (Hebrew Bible) and the cancelling of very real debts we could never pay (New Testament). Forgiving is never the goal of a relationship. Who makes a friend, marries a spouse, or has children with the goal of practicing more forgiveness? Although never the goal, forgiving is always an absolute essential in any relationship that grows in intimacy and trust. No forgiveness; no deepening and lasting intimacy.

I love the way Jeremiah, Ezekiel, Hosea, and several psalmists openly work through their need to *forgive* God for what God sometimes allows. I need those models. When we are honest, most of us must admit that it is imperative not only that God forgive us if our relationship is to remain intimate; it is also imperative that we forgive God for some of the things God allows in our personal lives and in the world. It does not matter that someday I might see that there was no better way for God to be God in our world: I live now, not someday.

Living in the now, I must forgive God for allowing us humans to invent the nuclear weapons that have haunted the entire existence of my life, my children's lives, my grandchildren's lives, and now my great-grandchildren's lives. On a personal level, I need to forgive God for allowing my wonderful, beautiful, hard-working, and faithful wife to develop the horrible Parkinson's brain disease. I need to forgive God for allowing the brutal, often denied, racist words, acts, and systems that haunt the lives of my biracial family. I find huge help in doing this through the models written and saved for us by Jewish people in the many Psalms and Prophets that include taking God to task for what God has allowed.

Thankfulness as an attitude and action that is appropriate, not only when we receive a gift or a perk, but also when we are having to trust God with a situation that is *bad*. Not that we must thank God for the evil that has been done, but we can thank God that God will never waste it. If we place it in God's hands, no matter how unjust and how wrong the situation, God will work toward ultimate good for those who are committed to loving God (Rom 8:28–39).

Covenant is a binding agreement between us and God for which God is willing to pay a higher cost, take more risk, and accept more responsibility than we do. The ancient world was filled with covenants, but the person with the lower status and lesser empowerment always took on the major risks, costs, and obligations of the covenant. The covenant-making God revealed in the Hebrew Bible always takes on the greatest risks, pays the highest costs, and assumes the deepest obligations in God's covenant with us humans. This strange content for the word *covenant* was enacted in the imagery of Genesis 15 when it is God, not Abraham, who passes between the two halves of the covenant-sacrifice. It is enacted again when Jesus declares that God is enacting a new covenant in the spilling of Jesus's life-blood on behalf of "many." To say it another way: "God so loved the world that God gave God's one and only son. . . ."

Patterns

The images reflecting patterns of God's interactions with humans is as important a gift from God through the Jewish people as are the content-laden words. Again, a few of many possible examples follow.

I am in the *Wilderness* right now, but I am bound for God's *Promised Land.* Followers of Jesus have used these images regularly through the centuries. The content comes from the Exodus narrative, the ministry of John the Baptist, and the initial temptations at the beginning of Jesus's ministry. All this content is a gift from God, through Jewish experiences with God.

The Old Testament gave us a clear pattern that most of us would just as soon ignore. Through the lives of people such as Naomi, Jeremiah, Ezekiel, and Hosea, we see that a believing and observant person of faith may still be a *suffering servant* in a bent, broken, and unjust world. Jesus filled this pattern full of even deeper meaning, but as 1 Peter 2:18–25 makes clear, the pattern did not stop with Jesus. Contrary to the "prosperity gospel" that presents a false "good news," claiming faith should end our suffering in this broken world, the genuine good news is that God suffers with us and will never waste our suffering. God allowed Jesus to be tortured and executed unjustly as God's *suffering servant.* We are not exempt from the suffering; we are included in the ultimate justice (Rom 8:17–18, Col 1:24, and 2 Tim 3:12).

Does anyone you know say, "I need to *take up my Cross*" or "I hope for a *resurrection* after this horrible event?" We use this imagery to speak of moving headlong into situations God seems to expect us not to run from, even though we know we cannot handle them on our own. We might owe the Romans for their expertise in turning crucifixion into a form of execution rarely rivalled for its horror and its terrifying enactment of military control. However, we owe the Jewish Jesus for trusting the God of Abraham, who was the only one who could save him from this horrendous execution (Heb 5:7). And, we owe the Jewish writers of the New Testament for taking that event and recording it in a manner that helps us know God better and gives us an image for trust in the worst of circumstances.

The cross of the New Testament is not a pretty jewel around the neck or in the sanctuary; rather, it is the symbol of trusting God in the face of the hell we humans visit upon one another—and finding out that the God who seems to be absent isn't absent after all. God is a God of final resurrection and life.

Life is a *journey, a road, a pathway, a way*—all images that imply that life really is moving toward an important goal, but must be lived day by day and step by step. Proverbs highlights this imagery throughout. Long ago I was struck by my wife's wisdom as she reflected on this imagery in Psalm 119:105. She said, "Ron, have you ever thought about the fact that the picture here is of someone in the dark, walking on a path with a small torch providing light for perhaps one or two steps ahead. Isn't that the kind of guidance we usually receive from God?" I have since noted a few commentators making similar suggestions, but her insight came from daily life, rather than from a book. This image for daily step-by-step living and guidance is embedded in the goal-oriented relationship with God described in by Old and New Testament writers.

What many Christians call "the Sacraments," especially *Baptism* and *Communion*, are extensions of patterns developed in the Jewish experience prior to Jesus. Hebrews 6:1–2 reminds us that baptism in the name of Jesus is embedded in the "baptisms" or "washings" (plural) that were practiced by the priests prior to Jesus. All four Gospels remind us that the baptism Jesus first experienced himself and then taught flowed directly from the ministry of the great prophet John the Baptist.

Some Christians call it "the Eucharist," some "the Communion," some "the Lord's Supper," and some "the Lord's Table." The church I belong to also often further identifies it as "Jesus's Open Table, where Jesus is the Host." Whatever your faith community calls it, it is important to remember that, according to every Gospel narrative, it began as a celebration of the Jewish Passover. Not only was the Passover the event Jesus was celebrating with his "faith-family" of Jewish disciples, the Hebrew Bible was the source of the all the content Jesus drew upon as he filled the ancient pattern with renewed meaning—"remember," "covenant," "new covenant," "forgiveness," "eat," "drink," and "blood of the covenant" all draw their content from Jesus's intentional patterning after the Old Testament narrative. The Psalm they sang as they left the supper would have been sung in various homes across Jerusalem that year as families and friends concluded their annual Passover celebration (Matt 26:30).

WE OWE THE JEWISH PEOPLE FOR MODELING CENTURIES OF FAITHFULNESS.

It is not just for revelation prior to Jesus, and for the blessings those of us who follow Jesus received from the first-century events: we also owe the later Jewish people for models of faithfulness toward God, despite persecutions and injustices. Preachers love to use examples of Christians who stood up faithfully to persecution at various points during the centuries. We are less likely to mention that many Jewish people stood faithfully as they endured persecutions enacted by Christians, even though the numbers seem to be clearly weighted in favor of the Jewish people.

I find it difficult to even write the next words, but truth must be confessed. Many Jewish people went to their death during the Holocaust praying "The LORD is Our God, the LORD is one. . . . Love the LORD God with all your heart, all your mind, and all your being," while "Christians" turned the gas valves and drove the trains. Simultaneously, most Christians all over Europe and all over the world either supported, accommodated, or ignored this horror. I am humbled by, and I wish to emulate if I ever must, the many martyrs of the Holocaust and of the Inquisition who went into torture and death taking upon themselves the Shema (faithfulness to and hope in the One God).

It has been not only during persecution, but in daily life patterns that many Jewish people have modelled honoring and trusting God through the centuries since Jesus. This included everyday family life and child-rearing. I want to insist that we Christians honor the faithfulness of the *average* Jewish worshipper, who is neither heroic nor a scholar, just as we honor the faithfulness of the *average* Christian worshipper, who is neither heroic nor a scholar. To push the point a step further, I personally know Jewish people who do not believe that Jesus is God's unique Son, who in some respects live more godly and giving lives—more *Christ-like lives* (my words, not theirs)—than I live.

Some Jewish people have also been willing to pay huge costs to support, and often lead, in social justice causes. For example, the 1960's Civil Rights Movement in the United States often involved Black Christians and Jews walking arm in arm into the clubs, dogs, and guns wielded by *white Christian* policemen, supported in their actions by their white church and their white pastor.

We are also indebted to Jewish people for writings that encourage a godly spirituality from which we who follow Jesus can learn a lot. A modern source of deeply touching everyday spiritual faithfulness is available in Rachel Naomi Remen's *My Grandfather's Blessings*. I would have loved to sit at his feet with her. From a generation earlier, Abraham Joshua Heschel's *God in Search of Man* challenges us to quit whining about how we humans must be so diligent in searching for a relationship with God and to recognize that God is far more diligently searching for a relationship with us. True, I experience God as *absent* sometimes in our relationship; far more often, God experiences me as *absent* in our relationship, as God pleads for me to return and open my eyes and arms to his loving outreach. I am relatively sure the same is true in your relationship with God. I am grateful for this Jewish sister and this Jewish brother, who with different styles remind me of this reality.

WE OWE THE JEWISH PEOPLE FOR SHOWING US THAT GOD HONORS TRUTH, TEARS, TURNING, AND TRUSTING.

Truth, Tears, Turning, and Trusting—a pattern we owe the Jewish people that is so central that it had to be where this chapter began and now concludes. Until we honestly confess and lament Christian history toward the Jewish people, there are blessings those of us who wish to follow Jesus will never be able to receive. Throughout the Old Testament narratives, there are times when the prophetic call for people who wish for more of God's blessings is clear—begin with confessing and lamenting, which means start acknowledging the truth and let the appropriate tears flow.

The New Testament is filled with the same message, beginning with John the Baptist, continuing through Jesus and the writers of the New Testament letters, and concluding with the "Letter to the Seven Churches" we call *Revelation*. Nothing can replace our need for truth and honest tears about our past if we wish our future to be "God with us" in relating to Jewish people. These steps can then be followed by turning from the ways church doctrines and interpretation of Scriptures continue to support anti-Semitism and turning toward trusting in the Jewish Jesus we Christians claim God appointed as our Lord and Savior.

11

Can Followers Of Jesus Move Beyond The Church's Anti-Semitism?

Can I? Can You?

MOVING TOWARD TRUTH, TEARS, TURNING, AND TRUSTING

ONLY WITH THE HELP of Jewish people can we Christians even begin to answer the question that titles this chapter. If we are to move successfully toward Truth, Tears, Turning, and Trusting, we must learn to listen when Jewish people speak to us. Certainly, this cannot mean agreeing with every critique of what we who follow Jesus trust to be true. It does, however, require listening to and learning from Jewish people, with humble hearts. The only proper response when a Jewish person tells me that what I said was anti-Semitic speech or that something I did was an anti-Semitic act is to listen, breathe deeply, and begin an honest self-examination. That is something our history as Christians has shown far too little of.

Unlike Paul, John, Luke, and Matthew, we now have a long church history replete with persecution of Jewish people to face up to. When they wrote, they had no idea that church history, and much of world history, was going to be dominated by anti-Semitism and anti-Judaism for more than seventeen centuries. They would have been horrified to know that this tragic history would often be justified using their words. We cannot expect these writers, who could never have imagined centuries of "Christian" Empires, to tell us all we need to know 2,000 years later concerning how followers of Jesus should relate to Jewish people who do not believe that Jesus was or is their Messiah, but we can ask how people with the basic values and worldview of these New Testament writers might approach our current situation. These were writers who believed that God is the God of real history and a God who responds to the changes in human history.

For those of us who believe that God's Holy Spirit was in fact empowering the New Testament writers as they wrote, it seems clear to me that we should understand that, if they were writing today, they would say some things quite differently from the way they wrote prior to the past 1,900 years of history. To fail to understand this truth is to fail to understand the vibrancy of inspiration as it was presented, and as it was continually and creatively reapplied, over and over again to new situations, in both the Old Testament and the New Testament literature.

If Paul were writing now, surely, he would be irate that his warning in Romans 11:11–16 to potentially anti-Semitic Roman followers of Jesus has been mostly ignored for 1,900 years of church history, while his critique of his fellow Jews has been used in ways that he would never countenance. I suspect he would now be scathing concerning Christian treatment of Jews.

Similarly, I do not doubt that the writer of John's Gospel would certainly use some term different from "the Jews" if he, as a Jewish person himself, were writing today after the two millennia of misuse of his materials by the church. Perhaps he would speak of "Jesus's peers" or "Jesus's brothers," or "the religious hierarchy," or "Jesus's fellow church leaders" ("church"—*qahal* in Hebrew and *ekklesia* in Greek originally meant "assembly" or "gathering," without necessarily implying "Christian"). Both proudly Jewish, John and Paul would find it a tragedy to discover that their words meant to honor what God has done through Jesus have been used to encourage hatred of Jesus's Jewish people and to distance Jesus himself from his Jewishness.

This tragedy continues to steal from us a much deeper understanding of the relationship between the Jewish Jesus and the One God of Israel and of Creation. Will we move past this horrid Christian past and its current expressions? I pray so. I hope so. There are some encouraging signs that we might, and there are more than a few discouraging signs that we might not. We can do so only when we lament again and again how deeply rooted in our practices and our theology sinful attitudes toward Jewish people have become.

WHAT TO DO? ONLY THE ONE GOD KNOWS, BUT WE MATTER IN GOD'S PROCESS.

I do not pretend to claim that I fully understand how God is bringing, or will bring, more peace between the two current realities of church and synagogue—Christianity and Judaism. As Amy-Jill Levine makes clear, many Christians, conservative and liberal alike, although for different reasons, still follow Augustine in seeing the continuing existence of Jews and Judaism as God's preservation of a negative foil to show how much more wonderful "true Christianity" is.[19] Jewish people are rightly insulted and, more importantly, they are deeply aware of the tragic historical consequences these theologies have engendered.

On the other hand, many Jewish people of the past and the present reject what the Jewish writers of the New Testament claim to be the central event and a major next step in God's great creation story, a story that maintains that Jesus was Israel's Messiah and that God invited Gentiles like me into the one family of God, based on God's covenant relationship with Abraham, as God moved it forward through Jesus.

It is easy to see why a person like me sees this inclusion through Jesus as such a wonderful truth claim. As a non-Jewish person, I am included in the offer of equally privileged status in God's ongoing revelation of God's purpose in history. I am no longer an outsider

19. Levine, Misunderstood Jew, 167–90.

to the main thrust of God's self-revelation in history (Eph 1:12–13, 2:11–12, and Rom 11:17–18).

Simultaneously, it is easy to see why what I trust is true about the relationship between God and Jesus, and what it means to the rest of us, is and was seen by those who do not believe Jesus to be God's Messiah for Israel as a damaging threat to Jewish faithfulness and even to Jewish existence. If privileged status in God's active pursuit of God's purpose in history has moved beyond the religious community created by the specificity of the Torah, and keeping Torah is now open in a new way to all ethnicities and cultures through trust in what God has done in God's relationship with Jesus, why continue to keep Torah in the manner that was demanded before Jesus? Of course that was (and is) seen as a huge threat to Jewish culture, Jewish ethnicity, and Jewish faithfulness.

If there is no longer any *privileged* relationship with God available through such faithful boundary keeping, will ethnic heritage and pride be enough to keep the ethnic culture and faithfulness alive? This has been a very real and understandable issue for many Jewish people through the centuries. I personally do not believe that God would ever allow the Jewish heritage to disappear, but it is easy to see why the fear exists. Just listen to what many Christians around the world keep saying!

Ironically, Christian sins have helped provide some of the glue that binds many Jewish people to their ethnicity as the "us" who can never trust "them." I have known several Jewish people who told me explicitly that their main Jewish identity had little to do with God or faith, but was instead defined by being "not Christian." Sadly, the "you should never trust them" has proved an accurate assessment of many of us Christians where Jewish people have been concerned.

It might be true that God has used these Christian sins to preserve Jewishness through many centuries of abuse and oppression. It is not true that this excuses horrendous sinfulness on the part of us Christians who claim to be following a Jewish man named Jesus. I think if I were Jewish, the historical reality of Christian oppression alone would cause me to hang on tightly to my Jewishness, no matter what. I hope that I would still somehow have come to trust that I could be Jewish and be a follower of Jesus, although I know that many Jewish people and many Christian people alike would tell me this is not possible. In fact, I write this knowing that the statements in this paragraph, and the following ones you are about to read, are likely to be some of the most frustrating in this book to many Jews and to many Christians—for very different reasons.

Nevertheless, I would be dishonest, and I don't think we will ever more forward if we cannot learn to be truthful in the process, not to note three realities in my experience. First, I do have several Jewish friends who are followers of Jesus, while self-identifying deeply as Jewish and hardly at all as "Christian." I am not talking about the "Messianic Jews" who openly and often loudly identify as "Christians." In fact, they sometimes arrogantly self-identify as the most authentic Jews, as well as the most authentic Christians on the planet. I am speaking of several friends—and I expect there are quite a few others I do not know—who find being identified as "Christian" to be very distasteful, but who have nonetheless experienced what they understand to be powerful experiences with God and with the risen human Jesus. These experiences leave them in the limbo of being distrusted by most Christians and most Jews alike.

Second, in an attempt at transparency, even when it causes tension, I need to acknowledge that, on the one hand I do not feel compelled to proselytize Jewish people because I am certain God is a gracious God, searching throughout the world for good-hearted people who faithfully seek God and love their fellow humans. On the other hand, I do wish that Jewish people could find a way to claim Jesus more fully as their own. I think we would all learn so much more in that process, and perhaps we could all draw even closer to God in that process. This wish flows from my conviction that the inclusive heart of God does not preclude a specific historical goal toward which God is at work—a goal that historically runs from the creation of "male and female in the image of God," through Abraham and Sarah, Moses and Miriam, Jesus, and a future in which all of this will be brought to fulfillment in God's renewal of creation and of humans, who will corporately be God's forever human family, and individually finally completed into the image of God as humans are meant to be. I see nothing that makes an inclusive heart and an exclusive historical process incompatible for a gracious and purposeful God.

Third, I personally find the fact that many of my Jewish friends and acquaintances deny that a Jewish person can remain Jewish and trust her or his experiences with Jesus at the same time to be both very understandable and not very understandable. I also find it personally painful because it deeply pains several of my dearest friends.

On the not understandable side is the reality that a Jewish person can practice almost anything else—atheism, communism, Buddhist meditation, and Ashram participation, faith in nothing other than Israeli nationalism or American nationalism, and still be recognized as "Jewish" by most Jewish people. But to practice following Jesus seems to be the one life decision that means being denied the privilege of recognition as a fellow Jew in the minds of many Jewish people.

On the understandable side is the fact that atheists and Buddhists have never threatened to annihilate Jews, nor have they participated in forced "conversions." (The same cannot be said about atheistic communism.) Also on the understandable side is the perceived threat to Jewish faith and culture when Jewish people decide to follow Jesus, because "Christianity" and "Western Culture" have now been so intertwined for so many centuries.

Although I know there are major differences, in some ways this concern seems similar to the very understandable reaction of many black friends when my black son-in-law decided to marry my white daughter. My daughter and my new son experienced love and commitment to one another. Far too many white friends and relatives were skeptical, due to deep-seated prejudices most of them preferred not to own up to. On the other hand, several black friends experienced the understandable fear that the black culture was losing yet another talented, wise, and gifted black man. In this case that was a completely unfounded fear, but a very understandable one. Can it ever be an unfounded fear where Jewish people and Jesus are concerned?

What to do? There is no easy solution between followers of Jesus and many Jewish people! How could there be? We trust in the same God and we serve the same God. Yet some of us trust that when God begins the coming age, we will all find out that Jesus is God's Messiah and central to God's forgiveness and God's future plans for all of us. Others of us are sure that Jesus was not God's Messiah and is not important to our present or future relationship with God.

SO, WHAT DO WE DO?

As I said, I do know that the previous few paragraphs can cause tension and be alienating to many Jewish people. Again, in an attempt at transparency, it concerns me far less that those same paragraphs might also cause tension and be alienating to some Christians, but I hope not to you, if you are a Christian reader. I hope many of you will join me in making it our goal to speak and live in a way that makes it clear that we are repentant for our sins against the Jews, we lament our history toward the Jews, and we want to grow up and act like people who serve a great and gracious God. In short, we want to honor the faithful and loving challenge presented to us by a faithful and loving Jewish human named Jesus.

To any Jewish person who might read this book, I say, "It makes me sad that we who claim to follow Jesus have done so much harm to you and those Jewish people who preceded you. It makes me sad that I have, and probably continue to, hurt you at times. I do not want to add to the hurt we Christians have caused you. If things I have written hurt, I am sorry. I just don't know how to move forward, apart from openness and honesty and practicing listening to one another and learning from one another."

So, what to do? I cannot deny that I believe God has a wonderfully inclusive heart. I cannot deny that I think following Jesus is not a religion, but a participation in God's exclusive goal of a special self-revelation in human history, which is to make humans, male and female, into the image of God as God's forever human family. I think Jesus is the first of many humans to be "completed/perfected" (the theme of the letter of Hebrews and of Romans 8:28–39 in the New Testament, as well as of another book I am working on) in God's great creation project.

So, what to do? As much as I am able, I want to understand why Jewish people, both in Jesus's time and now, see the New Testament claims concerning what God has done through Jesus as very threatening. I also want to acknowledge that it is easy to see that many of the things Christians have said and done with these texts over the past 1,900 years have vastly increased that threat.

It seems important to reiterate here that the issue of God's wide graciousness is not just a Jewish–Christian issue. There have been people from every background and every religious context who have been God-seekers and who have courageously lived for God and for good. Many Christians, and many Jews, have always believed that God searches the entire earth to find those whose hearts are turned toward God. Biblically speaking, this is the pre-Judaism, and certainly pre-Christian, covenant of God's care for all of humanity and all of creation—sometimes called the "Noahic covenant" or the "Adamic covenant."

But my emphasis is specifically on the relationship between Jews and Christians. It is about the unavoidable tension raised between Christians and Jews by the claim that the relationship between God and Jesus is deeply embedded in God's covenant history with the Jewish people. It is an attempt to confess, lament, and repent concerning how badly we followers of Jesus have handled this tension, and it is a plea that we must do better by growing in our trust in God and one another.

How can God move beyond our apparent historical impasse? Only God knows, but I am convinced that God *does* know.

As one whose hope for humanity lies precisely with the New Testament claims concerning Jesus, I cannot take it lightly that others are adamantly certain that I am wrong. I cannot betray or water down my trust in what God has done through Jesus in order to be like-minded.

What I can do is agree with all people of Jewish ethnicity that Christians need to do a lot of soul-searching. Our history is horrid with respect to Jewish people. I can honor and respect the faithfulness of many Jewish people and work together on the many things we value in common. I can also acknowledge openly that sometimes I learn more about the real historical Jesus, how he lived, and the context of what he said from authors such as Amy-Jill Levine and Daniel Boyarin than I do from reading the commentaries and theological tomes of many Christian scholars.

I can be insistent with fellow followers of Jesus that we honor the many faithful Jewish people who do not believe that Jesus was or is the Jewish Messiah, but who express a covenant relationship with God that sometimes puts the way I express my—and my fellow Christians express their—relationship with the One God to shame. This has been true throughout the Current Era. I can celebrate how much I learn from, how deeply humbled I am by the relationship with God, and the understanding of God, expressed by such Jewish writers as Abraham Joshua Heschel, Pinchas Lapide, Etty Hillesum, Jules Isaac, and Rachel Naomi Remen. I can do my best to listen to and hear the astute insights of our local Rabbi, who graciously offers his time and wisdom to me. I can also insist that we Christians honor the faithfulness of the *average* Jewish worshipper, who is neither heroic nor a scholar, just as we honor the faithfulness of the *average* Christian worshipper who is neither heroic nor a scholar.

If ever I must, I can pray that I will emulate the faithfulness of the many martyrs of the Holocaust and of the Inquisition whose faith certainly shone brighter than that of many Christians during those times. I can continue to acknowledge the godly, gracious, giving lives of many Jewish people, who under less trying circumstances practice goodness and justice in our world.

I am confident that the prophet Isaiah (see Isa 19:18–25, 49:6, and 56:3–6) was correct in claiming that the "One God" has God's "one family" goal figured out in ways that none of the rest of us can quite yet imagine. Without claiming that I know how God will do it, I am certain that it will be with more love and truth and grace than either our conservative, our liberal, our liberation, or our "new perspective" Christian theologies can seem to muster. Unlike us, the "One God of Israel" seems quite capable of having one very exciting and very exclusive historical purpose, while simultaneously expressing one very huge inclusive heart. Since we probably cannot imagine the "how," we should leave it to God, while doing our best to learn to better love and honor one another. I am sure that the "Jesus way" means that we Christians who claim to follow the Jewish

Jesus had better learn to love our Jewish sisters and brothers much more clearly than we have usually managed to do—or face God's continuing anger and frustration for our failure to do so.

Meanwhile, those of us who believe the New Testament story to be true, that God's covenant relationship with the Jewish human Jesus really was the fulfillment of Israel's history and the opening up of the family of God to God's future for blessing all nations through the covenant relationship with Abraham, must take seriously that all of the New Testament writers, many to whom they wrote, and Jesus the Messiah of whom they wrote, were fully committed to the "One God" of Israel.

What to do? The more we take seriously that Jesus really was a first-century Jew, the more we take seriously that Jesus was really a first-century human, the more we will find it necessary and liberating to focus on the New Testament emphasis that the relationship between Jesus and God really is about "for God so loved *the world*." This focus will continue to move us toward more truth, tears, turning, and trusting.

Bibliography

Bauckham, Richard. *Jesus and the Eyewitnesses: The Gospels as Eyewitness Testimony.* Grand Rapids: Wm. B. Eerdmans, 2006.

Boyarin, Daniel. *The Jewish Gospels: The Story of the Jewish Christ.* New York: The New Press, 2012.

————. *A Radical Jew: Paul and the Politics of Identity.* London: University of California Press, 1997.

Carroll, James. *Constantine's Sword: The Church and the Jews.* New York: Mariner Books, 2002.

Dostoevsky, Fyodor, *The Brothers Karamazov.* Translated by Constance Garnett. 1952. *Dostoevsky.* Great Books of the Western World. London: Britannica, 1978.

Dunn, James D. G., *Jews and Christians: The Parting of the Ways: AD 70–135.* Grand Rapids: Wm. B. Eerdmans, 1999.

Ehrman, Bart D. *How Jesus Became God: The Exaltation of a Jewish Preacher from Galilee.* New York: HarperCollins, 2015.

Heschel, Abraham Joshua. God in Search of Man: A Philosophy of Judaism. New York: American Book–Stratford, 1955.

Hill, Wesley. *Paul and the Trinity: Persons, Relations, and the Pauline Letters.* Grand Rapids: Wm. B. Eerdmans, 2015.

Hurtado, Larry. *How on Earth Did Jesus Become a God? Historical Questions about Earliest Devotion to Jesus.* Grand Rapids: Wm. B. Eerdmans, 2005.

Isaacs, Jules. *Jesus and Israel.* 1951. Translated by Sally Gran. New York: Holt, Rinehart and Winston, 1971.

Jocz, Jacob. *The Jewish People and Jesus Christ: The Relationship Between Church and Synagogue.* Grand Rapids: Baker Book House, 1979.

————. *The Jewish People and Jesus Christ After Auschwitz: A Study in the Controversy Between Church and Synagogue.* Grand Rapids: Baker Book House, 1981.

Kendi, Ibram X. *How To Be An Anti-Racist.* New York: One World, 2019.

Lapide, Pinchas, *The Resurrection of Jesus: A Jewish Perspective*. Minneapolis: Augsburg, 1983.

Levenson, John D. *Resurrection and the Restoration of Israel: The Ultimate Victory of the God of Life*. New Haven: Yale University, 2006.

Levine, Amy-Jill. The Misunderstood Jew: The Church and the Scandal of the Jewish Jesus. New York: HarperOne, 2006.

Lewis, C. S. *Christian Reflections*. Grand Rapids: Wm. B. Eerdmans, 1967.

Luther, Martin, *The Jews and Their Lies*. 1543. Reedy, W.V.: Liberty Bell Publications, 2004.

Remen, Rachel Naomi, *My Grandfather's Blessings*. New York: Riverhead Books, 2000.

Spong, John Shelby, *A New Christianity for a New World: Why Traditional Faith is Dying & How a New Faith is Being Born*. New York: HarperCollins, 2002.

Stark, Rodney *For the Glory of God*. Princeton: Princeton University Press, 2003.

———. *The Rise of Christianity*. San Francisco: HarperSanFrancisco, 1997.

Stevenson, Bryan. We Need to Talk about Injustice. *TED Talks*: https://www.youtube.com/watch?v=c2tOp7OxyQ8. 2012.

Vermes, Geza. *Jesus the Jew: A Historian's Reading of the Gospels*. Philadelphia: Fortress, 1973.

Weitzman, Steven. *The Origin of the Jews: The Quest for Roots in a Rootless Age*. Princeton: Princeton University Press, 2017.

Wright, N. T. *Paul and the Faithfulness of God*. Minneapolis: Fortress, 2013.

———. *The Resurrection of the Son of God*. Minneapolis: Fortress, 2003.

Index

Made in the USA
Coppell, TX
14 November 2020

41375884R00085